Exceptional Care for Your Valued Client

Bob Nicoll, M.A.
LuAnn Buechler, CMP, M.S.

Bronwyn Emery Ashbaker

Exceptional Care for Your Valued Client

Exceptional Care for Your Valued Client

First published in 2011 by:

Ecademy Press
48 St Vincent Drive, St Albans,
Hertfordshire, AL1 5SJ
info@ecademy-press.com
www.ecademy-press.com

Printed and Bound by: Lightning Source in the UK and USA

Cover Design and Book Typesetting by: Catalyst Design

Printed on acid-free paper from managed forests.
This book is printed on demand, so no copies will be remaindered or pulped.

ISBN-978-1-907-722240

The right of Bob Nicoll to be identified as the author of this work has been asserted in accordance with sections 77 and 78 of the Copyright Designs and Patents Act 1988.

A CIP catalogue record for this book is available from the British Library.

All rights reserved. No part of this publication may be reproduced in any material form (including photocopying or storing in any medium by electronic means and whether or not transiently or incidentally to some other use of this publication) without the written permission of the copyright holder except in accordance with the provisions of the Copyright, Designs and Patents Act 1988. Applications for the Copyright holders written permission to reproduce any part of this publication should be addressed to the publishers.

The purpose of this book is to educate and entertain. The author and Ecademy Press shall have neither liability nor responsibility to any person or entity with respect to any loss or damage caused, or alleged to have been caused, directly or indirectly, by the information contained in this book.

If you do not wish to be bound by the above, you may return this book to the place where you purchased it or to the publisher for a full refund.

©Bob Nicoll, M.A.
LuAnn Buechler, CMP, M.S.
Bronwyn Emery Ashbaker

Praise for

Exceptional Care for Your Valued Client

"If your new clients have increased, yet your client list is the same size, then this is the book for you. Bob, LuAnn and Bronwyn show you examples of everyday common mistakes that produce the opposite of what we desire in customer service. By learning how to reframe our words and our thoughts, we can create a "CAN DO" environment that empowers us to solve our client needs and allows us to demonstrate they are valued. Happy clients are loyal clients! Growing AND retaining your client base is how you move forward. As a business consultant, I will be recommending this book to all of my clients."

**Amy Kilpatrick, President and Co-Founder,
Nspired Networking Enterprises, LLC**

"**Exceptional Care for Your Valued Client** raises the bar when it comes to current thinking and ideals regarding customer service. With just one read-through it will shift your paradigms in a way that will proactively position you and your business for success."

**Dr. Ivan Misner,
NY Times Bestselling author
and Founder of BNI and Referral Institute**

Exceptional Care for Your Valued Client

"The first time I met Bob and heard his Remember the Ice story, I knew he had a paradigm shifting message to share. In **Exceptional Care for Your Valued Client**, Bob, LuAnn and Bronwyn have set a new standard for businesses on caring for their most precious commodity--their clients. This book will change your perspective on caring for your clients.

It changed mine."

Thomas Power, Chairman, Ecademy
www.ecademy.com

"Exceptional Care of your customers and clients means you create signature moments that propel them back to your business forever. Give them exceptional care and they return the favor. Blueprint your business by this book— expressing exceptional care clearly and powerfully—and discover how you receive a Work Positive lifestyle!"

Dr. Joey Faucette, Work Positive:
How to Work Positive in a Negative World,
www.ListentoLife.org

"**Exceptional Care for Your Valued Client** shows us how metaphysical ideas applied to business can transform and enrich us and those who work with us."

Barnet Bain, Owner,
Chance to Choice Solutions, Producer,
"What Dreams May Come,
The Celestine Prophecy"

"**Exceptional Care for Your Valued Client**" is an excellent book for anyone committed to providing the best possible service for their clients. This book will help you communicate effectively with your customers and your staff, making it easier than ever for your business to grow and thrive. You may be reminded of some things you already know, but when you ask yourself, "Am I DOING that?" you will understand the real value of this book."

Robert MacPhee, Founder and President, Heart Set, Inc. Author: "Manifesting of Non-Gurus", Founding Member: Transformational Leadership Council

"Exceptional client care. What a great idea! What a rare experience nowadays! Everyone talks about delivering great service but so few actually do. If there was ever a need for help with this subject, it's now! You will get fresh insights from THE master of word choice, Bob Nicoll. Bob combines his talent for powerful articulation with practical ways to deliver the kind of service that sets you apart from the rest. Read this book!!"

Mark Taylor, Executive Director, BNI Houston East

Exceptional Care for Your Valued Client

Contents

Acknowledgements i
Foreword iii
Introduction 1

SECTION 1
The First/Worst Words to Eliminate and Replace – Know Your (K)nots 3

Chapter 1
Why Make the Effort to Provide Exceptional Care for Your Valued Client? 5

Chapter 2
There is Power in the Clarity of Your Articulation™ 15

Chapter 3
Remember the Ice and Untie Your (K)nots 25

Chapter 4
The Pitfalls of Tying "Do" Up In (K)nots 39

Chapter 5
Strangling the Host 55

Chapter 6
No Means No 71

Section 1 Exercises
Raising the bar on "(K)notty Word" Awareness 87

SECTION 2
Learning How to Speak and Act to Empower Yourself AND Your Client 91

Chapter 7
Learning How You Learn in Order to Re-Learn 93

Chapter 8
What's Wrong With Always Right? 107

Chapter 9
Shoulds, Absolutes, and More Words to Watch Out For 117

Chapter 10
Respectful Elegance via your Employees 125

Chapter 11
Respectful Elegance and the Power of Self-Esteem 135

Chapter 12
Best Practices: Client Service Words and Behavior 145

Exceptional Care for Your Valued Client

Section 2 Exercises
Learning How to Speak and Act to Empower Yourself AND Your Client..........155

SECTION 3
The Whole Package: Delivery and Results..159

Chapter 13
Physiology and Congruency 161

Chapter 14
Building a Framework of Rapport..175

Chapter 15
Forget the Price, Keep the Value..185

Section 3 Exercises
The Whole Package: Delivery and Results..197

SECTION 4
The Difference is in the Details..199

Chapter 16
It takes Time to Deliver Value...201

Chapter 17
The ABCs of Emotions. How Dare You Have an Attitude? 213

Chapter 18
Circling the Situation to Avoid Circling the Drain...225

Section 4 Exercises
The Difference is in the Details..233

SECTION 5
Where Do You Go From Here? Accountability & Action Create the Paradigm....237

Chapter 19
Old-Fashioned Ideas have New Fangled Appeal 239

Chapter 20
The Next Logical Step: Doing the Next Right Thing 249

Section 5 Exercises
Where Do You Go From Here? Accountability & Action Create the Paradigm....257

BIOGRAPHIES 259

Acknowledgements

Exceptional Care for Your Valued Client: *Customer Service from a Remember the Ice Perspective* is a subject I have wanted to explore and expound on for quite some time. The area of customer service and business relationships has at its core a unique blend of drive, compassion and empowering articulation. Raising awareness of both the demise of service in many areas, as well as the need for more of that empowering word choice sprinkled with Respectful Elegance, is the heartbeat of this book.

My friend and fellow BNI colleague, LuAnn Buechler contributed enormously to the content of this work. Her 30 years of exemplary experience in the Hospitality industry lend poignancy and compassion to her contributions. Thank you, LuAnn for your elegant signature.

I want to acknowledge the dedication, talent and extraordinary skills of Bronwyn Emery Ashbaker, my Developmental Editor. Her contributions of time, energy, insight and guidance for the project are unparalleled.

Thank you so much to my publisher, Ecademy Press and specifically Mindy Gibbins-Klein for her wisdom and guidance, and belief in the message. A big thank you to London based Mitch Herber and his staff at Catalyst Design, for the layout and overall design; and to my friend Mohamed Dobrova of Un1que Designs in Anchorage, Alaska for the concept and design of the ice-cubes for the cover.

A special thank you to all of the supporters, students, fans and friends who find themselves in the middle of a conversation; about to say a "(k)notty word"; realize it: stop—and reframe it; while looking around to see if Bob heard them. What a supreme compliment. Thank you for hearing the message of eradicating the "(k)notty words" and replacing them. I smile more and more each day when I see that happen. That behavior tells me that the message: There is Power in the Clarity of your Articulation; is developing a strong following, and for that I am especially grateful.

Exceptional Care for Your Valued Client

Foreword

by Ivan Misner
NY Times Bestselling Author and Founder of BNI® and Referral Institute®

It was during the 2007 BNI® (Business Network International) International Directors' Conference that I met long-time BNI member Bob Nicoll for the first time. It was then that I had the pleasure of talking with Bob about his recently developed empowering word choice program: *Remember the Ice*.

I agreed to have a look at Bob's program and a few weeks after the Conference I sat down and studied the material. At first I thought the title was a bit obscure. However, when I listened to the CD and heard the simple yet impactful short story about changing the word choice on a sign to encourage customers to buy ice, I was intrigued. I was quite interested in the significant shift in customer behavior and the dramatic increase in sales that occurred, all based on a simple change of words.

I quickly became a fan of Bob's unique message. Just prior to the 2008 release of his first book, *Remember the Ice and Other Paradigm Shifts*, I interviewed Bob on the Official BNI Podcast (episode #63) to discuss how his powerful concept *There is Power in the Clarity of Your Articulation*™ could be greatly beneficial to BNI members worldwide.

In that interview, I stated how rare it is for me to highlight books on the BNI Podcast; however I felt Bob's concept integrated very well into BNI and that it would surely help BNI members in their businesses as well as in their BNI groups. I believe the book is a critical tool in enhancing verbal and written messages and helping people use empowering word choices to attract the life they desire.

Now, three years later, Bob has teamed up with fellow BNI Director, LuAnn Buechler, as well as Developmental Editor, Bronwyn Emery Ashbaker, to bring us **Exceptional Care for Your Valued Client** – the second installment in the *Remember the Ice* Series.

Exceptional Care for Your Valued Client

Bob, LuAnn, and Bronwyn are committed to one main objective: *Shifting the concept of Customer Service to Providing Exceptional Care.* Providing Exceptional Care means that when our customers and clients call our business with questions or assistance needs, we can rest assured that they are in good hands because we know they are being connected with a member of our *Exceptional Care Team.*

The three co-authors of this book are a truly dynamic team who combine their unique individual skills, backgrounds, and expert knowledge to provide a smorgasbord of fresh, cutting-edge, powerfully-effective concepts that will help any business, large or small, provide *Exceptional Care* to customers and clients. LuAnn brings an extensive background of hospitality and event planning to the table. Bob's training in Counseling, Rational Behavior Therapy, Neuro-Associative Conditioning Systems, and the Psychophysiology of Words (I admit, I had to ask Bob to enlighten me on that one); is thorough and extensive. Finally, Bronwyn has a gift for bringing a voice to life on paper that mirrors the speaker's mindset, and it shows.

One very valuable aspect of *Exceptional Care* is the abundance of true stories we can learn critical lessons and strategies from. As the founder of BNI®, the world's largest word-of-mouth referral organization, and Referral Institute®, an internationally franchised referral training and consulting company, I have witnessed first-hand, time and time again, the power of sharing stories to get an impactful message across.

The overall message of the *Remember the Ice* Series is based on a simple story about a convenience store manager who increased his ice sales dramatically with minimal effort, and the reach of that story is now global. In addition to this story, which is found in Chapter 3, this book is full of compelling, real life stories; powerful examples of sticking with the basics and appreciating the rewards of persistent practice.

Exceptional Care has five sections and though each is capable of standing on its own, much like our thumb or any one of our fingers, when we embrace all five of them we can really get a grip on the subject of raising the bar when it comes to providing an exceptional level of client care.

In Chapter 5, we learn how eradicating two letters and an apostrophe can completely change the tenor of one's message. On the surface, it may sound "too good to be true." You may find yourself saying, as I did, "How can getting rid of the "(K)nots" in our language make such a big difference? It is too simple." Let me assure you, however, though it may be simple it is simultaneously comprehensive. Bob describes the basic concept of *Remember the Ice* as "the most simplistically complex concept you will ever come across." After my introduction to the program, I agree.

In Chapter 7, we are provided with some helpful information about that strange feeling we get when we attempt to change a longstanding behavior, like communication and word choice, and find ourselves being asked to eradicate words we have used thousands of times in favor of more empowering word choices. We learn that the internal tug-of-war over new word choice which appears to be a stumbling block at first; ultimately reveals itself as the next step in empowering both our communication skills and our ability to provide *Exceptional Care*.

Adding to the stories and "how to" material, this book contains essential, proven tools which can be put to use right away. For example, Chapter 12 showcases the best practice skills of LuAnn, a master at *"dealing with the angry, unreasonable, unyielding customer with the overblown sense of entitlement."*

Respectful Elegance, Framework of Rapport, Physiology and Congruency are the foundation of providing Exceptional Care. Bob and LuAnn's voices speak to the core of each business owner, employee, executive, and *Exceptional Care* team member (formerly known as customer service representatives). The difference is in the details and, with Bronwyn's talent and skill, this difference is articulated with a clarity and power that leads us to do the next right thing.

Effective communication and relationship building are at the forefront of BNI®, the organization I started over twenty-five years ago when I realized that word-of-mouth referral marketing is crucial in achieving business growth and success. The organization continues to grow and

Exceptional Care for Your Valued Client

prosper because BNI continues to serve its members (valued clients) by sharing specific, pertinent information designed to develop the skills and insight needed to sow the seeds and reap the rewards of successful networking.

Bob's mission with the *Remember the Ice* Series is to teach these very skills through empowering word choice and in *Exceptional Care for Your Valued Client*, Bob, LuAnn, and Bronwyn offer a veritable gold mine of knowledge that will benefit BNI members, business people, entrepreneurs, companies, and organizations across the globe. It has truly been an honor to endorse the *Remember the Ice* Series and to contribute the foreword for this book. I extend a wealth of gratitude and support to Bob, LuAnn, and Bronwyn as they embark on telling their compelling story of providing *Exceptional Care for Your Valued Client*.

They are well on their way to shifting the paradigm and I look forward to following their lead.

Ivan Misner, NY Times Bestselling Author and Founder of BNI® and Referral Institute®

Section 1

Introduction

It's raining.

It's raining "(K)notty Words".

He asked, *"Do you have your umbrella?"*

In the world of words and messages, my passion for linguistics and empowering word choices continues as a powerful heartbeat. It is also my umbrella to ward off the continual barrage of "(K)notty Words" I see and hear daily, in the world of Customer Service.

In October 2008, with the enormous help of Bronwyn Emery Ashbaker, my Developmental Editor, *Remember the Ice and Other Paradigm Shifts* was released. The book has a heartbeat in 37 countries; and through a large BNI and Ecademy network, the message continues to spread.

Communication is at the core of every personal moment, experience, transaction and interaction. Whether you are engaged in self-talk or presenting to a large audience, your word choices will have a significant impact on the results you achieve; and help you create a culture of confidence.

Remember the Ice is an easy to learn, yet comprehensive *empowering word choice* program that teaches you to enhance your communication skills with family members, friends, clients, co-workers — anyone who is important to you. It helps you stay focused on your task and accomplish your goals because you are conveying your message, and articulating your thoughts in a clear, precise manner. You eliminate confusion and gain confidence in your message and ultimately attract more of what you want.

The cornerstone of Remember the Ice is this truism:

*There is **Power** in the **Clarity** of your **Articulation**.* ™

The first book laid the foundation, or built the umbrella, teaching you how to achieve that clarity. Now in *Exceptional Care for Your Valued*

Exceptional Care for Your Valued Client

Client I have melded my passion for empowering word choice, my 35 plus years of study in Psychology and Counseling, and the insights of a delightful lady with 30 years experience creating exceptional care for her valued clients via her hospitality and event planning skills.

LuAnn Buechler is my colleague sharing this message of empowering word choice. I have known LuAnn since 2007 through our membership and Assistant Director roles in BNI (Business Network International) the world's largest word-of-mouth referral organization.

While playing a round of golf during the 2009 Get Connected Conference in St. Petersburg, FL, we began a conversation about how the "(K)notty Words" continue to display themselves in various customer service experiences. They ooze and spread like "going bad" cream cheese covering a stale bagel. LuAnn says, "There is no room for '(K)notty Words' in customer service." And I agree with her wholeheartedly.

While driving the cart down the third fairway – following a couple of stellar tee shots – we realized we had a message to convey, and decided right then to deliver it to you.

Providing Exceptional Care for Your Valued Client is one of several areas that the Remember the Ice umbrella covers; re-framing concepts for customer service messages falls neatly underneath it. On the horizon are more areas begging for an infusion of knowledge and understanding, including sales; marketing and advertising; parent/child communication; the fundamentals of empowering word choice for children, athletes and coaches; intimacy in relationships; and more.

*There is **Power** in the **Clarity** of your **Articulation**.* ™

For this book, we know:

*There is **Power** in the **Clarity** of **Providing Exceptional Care for Your Valued Client.***

So join us for some enlightening concepts and hands-on tools you can use immediately to enhance the Exceptional Care you are providing for *Your* Clients.

SECTION 1

The First/Worst Words to Eliminate and Replace – Know Your (K)nots

Chapter 1: Why Make the Effort to Provide Exceptional Care to Your Valued Client?

Chapter 2: There is Power in the Clarity of your Articulation™

Chapter 3: Remember the Ice and Untie your (K)nots

Chapter 4: The Pitfalls of Tying "Do" Up In (K)nots

Chapter 5: Strangling the Host

Chapter 6: No Means No

Exercises for Section 1

Exceptional Care for Your Valued Client

Section 1

Chapter 1

Why Make the Effort to Provide Exceptional Care for Your Valued Client?

Communication is the first and last word in customer service.

Your success or failure swings on your ability to communicate clearly, succinctly, tactfully, confidently, and congruently. It seems simple and obvious. I can picture you raising an eyebrow, thinking *"Okay, Bob, when are you going to tell me something new?"*

The concept that communication is at the core of all customer service may indeed be obvious to you. It may be the first lesson you learned in Business 101. It may be the first lesson you teach your employees. It may even be the one thing you try to hammer into their heads every day at every opportunity. Yet what is it in action, and how do you know when you are doing it well?

It's good to share the concept with your employees, remind them of it, point to a sign or poster on the wall that celebrates "communication" with some well-worn phrase, and even admonish them to practice "good communication" with your customers and clients. However, have you figured out how to teach it? Just what is this communication "it" everyone is talking about?

Communication is actually a complex arrangement of many parts, and developing it into something you do well requires awareness and vigilance. It seems simple because we are all born communicating in one way or another. Whether it's successful or ineffectual, we're all doing it.

Something else we all participate in is the exchange of goods and services. In one form or another, customer service is a part of every business. We know that to survive in business we need to provide everyone who walks through the door, calls on the phone or checks us out on the Internet with good customer service.

Exceptional Care for Your Valued Client

We all get to be customers, too, so we all learn to know good service when we see it, or rather, notice when it's absent. Customer service is so common it must be easy to define, right? You know when it's good and you sure as heck know when it's bad. But can you identify each of the components that went into its success or failure?

The key to providing **"Exceptional Care for Your Valued Client"** lies in being able to do just that: identify each piece of the communication puzzle, develop it, refine it, and use it properly to build a complete and empowering customer service program. If you are in business, your customers and clients are your most important reason for staying in business.

If you are motivated to learn something new about communication so you, too, can dramatically increase the standard of customer service your business provides, then you have come to the right place. Shifting your current view of customer service and changing your models and patterns of delivery, is what I call "shifting your paradigm." As you will see, raising the bar requires shifting the paradigm. It is the process that will elevate your customer service standards to that of providing **Exceptional Care for Your Valued Client**.

If you are sincere in your desire to change your current paradigm and revolutionize your business, keep reading. You will first need to change your perception, and I will show you why and how. If you are cynical and ready to challenge these notions as they unfold, have at it. Please, take every word, lesson and explanation I put forward here and test it out. I am always excited to hear what happens when people apply my concepts to their lives and businesses.

I am going to take you through the fundamentals of my cornerstone philosophy, "There is Power in the Clarity of Your Articulation," as shared and taught in my life-changing communication program "Remember the Ice and Other Paradigm Shifts." As I do so, I will show you how to apply each lesson to the world of customer service in a way that will show you, how empowering the shifts in your communication and customer service paradigms can be.

Section 1

I will show you exactly how to identify when you are communicating well, when you need to make better choices, and most importantly, how to apply the information in these pages so you can start making effective and powerful word choice work for you.

Until you are able to do that you will continue to offer the same kind of service you always have, be it good, bad or indifferent. If you are reading this book, chances are you suspect something in your organization needs to change, or you understand there is always room for improvement. Great customer service, or the ability to provide ***"Exceptional Care for Your Valued Client,"*** relies completely on great communication skills.

If you gauge your company's customer service skills by how well you meet quotas or the sum total of survey results, then you are missing the big picture. Whatever strides you think you are making will come to a swift end. Those tools have their uses, however, when you focus on information that tells you how to shut the barn door after the horses have run away, then you are putting yourself behind the competition. And we all know what it means when we're behind someone else: They get to be ahead. In business, that means they are the ones who win and get all the good customers.

Focus on the beginning point, the barn before the scene is disrupted. Be proactive. Gauge your company's customer service skills by a new set of standards. Take care of what you already have, and your customers will have no reason to be tempted away.

With this book I hope to show you that your beginning point in all things to do with customer service is communication. Start with providing ***"Exceptional Care for Your Valued Client"*** as your end goal, and you can expect rewarding and empowering payoffs all the way down the line.

Let's take a second to understand what a "good customer" is. Here is a list of attributes, in random order. Place them in the order of importance that makes the most sense to you.

Exceptional Care for Your Valued Client

- A good customer comes in, conducts his or her business, and leaves
- A good customer engages in conversation or small talk
- A good customer is a repeat customer
- A good customer has a lot of questions
- A good customer has very few or no questions
- A good customer pays on time
- A good customer brings other good customers to your door
- A good customer never complains, even when things go wrong
- A good customer points out problems and expects you to solve them

What did you put at the top of your list? If you led with "A good customer pays on time," then once again, you are missing the point. Yes, a good customer does pay on time, however I believe this attribute comes in behind "A good customer is a repeat customer" and "A good customer brings other good customers to your door." These two, placed ahead of the rest, remind us that repeat and expanded business are the most important goals; they bring in a lot more money than a single transaction, and frankly, that's what keeps your business alive. This book is about valued clients, which is a concept that encompasses *relationship*.

Relationship can take the shape of a customer who comes back every week for 10 years, or it can take the shape of a customer who is just passing through town or who stops by once every 10 years.

Regardless of the breadth and depth of the relationship potential you think you have with a customer or client, your goal with each and every one of them must be to make an impression, to stand out, and to create what I call a "Signature Moment" that makes your business memorable for all the right reasons.

A Signature Moment is an intentionally created experience which leaves the customer walking away with a positive thought, feeling, memory or acknowledgment about you, your employee or your business. It is that magic something that brings the customer walking back through your door time and time again. Your word choice and your communication skills make Signature Moments possible.

Section 1

The Signature Moment is the beginning of your relationship. If you forget to do that, you might as well go home for the night. We will explore signature moments in depth later in the book. For now, know that the key to creating them is – you guessed it – *communication*.

It's easy to see why you would want to create signature moments for local consumers and develop relationships with those who can return to hire your services with predictable regularity. You need and want them to come back, so you naturally make an effort to be the business they want to work with consistently.

The more transitory relationships can be a little harder to get behind, yet make no mistake: While the customer who is "just passing through" may have limited influence over other consumers in your town, remember that it's the 21st century, and he has the ability to influence overlapping consumer communities of hundreds and even thousands of people who rely on the Internet as a resource.

Consider this a precautionary tale, in case you have trouble identifying with the need to establish and maintain relationships with the people who walk through your front door, make an effort to call you on the phone, or choose to click on your web-site instead of a competitor's. The world is much smaller than it used to be. You may have the only import car dealership in your county, yet if you are unwilling to bend over backwards to get your customer exactly what she wants, like leather interior, seat warmers, and a DVD player for the kids, she will leave you in her dust, jump online and find what she wants somewhere else in the country.

Then she'll tell her neighbors what she did when you were unable to help, how great it was, and how happy she is with her new car. Later that day, she will take pictures of her new car and put them up on her Facebook and MySpace pages and brag about how resourceful she was in her search for the perfect car. Friends will ask how she did it and she will post her answers in great detail for all to see.

Next, she will write a glowing review on that other dealer's web site, the one that was so helpful, pointing out how you frustrated her so

Exceptional Care for Your Valued Client

much she had to turn to them for what she wanted, and will gush about their great service. Whether she spells it out or leaves it out, the implication will hang in the air that you were more than unsatisfactory; you were so bad that you drove her out of the county, maybe even out of the state to find what you failed to provide.

Then, she will jump on a different kind of review site, one designed for people who need help deciding where to buy their next car, and she will outline the process she chose and what led her to a different option all over again. Can you guess how many people she influenced in a single afternoon?

Every single person who interacts with you and your business has a voice, as well as a number of platforms from which to tell his or her story. Our current culture encourages individuals to use the Internet to reach out to communities of friends and consumers to either direct them to your front door or steer them away. The number of people who believe it is their duty to do so is growing.

Customer review sites like Yelp.com, Angieslist.com and Epinions.com are full of anecdotal evidence that can either elevate or condemn the reputation of a business. Reviewers, who, on a whole, represent the average consumer, base the way they rate a business and whether they recommend others to use it on personal experiences.

Their first-person reviews have nothing to do with company policies, projected ROI statistics, survey results, corporate dictums, market shares, or any other behind-the-scenes information. Their reviews are based entirely on how it felt to be your customer. Their "customer experience" is what matters most to them.

Very few customers care why a shelf in your store is nearly empty; they just care that it is nearly empty. Even fewer people care that the manager's baby was up all night with a fever, or a pipe burst in his house, or the car broke down on the way in; they just care that the manager was short-tempered and abrasive.

Section 1

On this kind of web site with consumer-generated reviews, the comments are on a par with what you would hear from your best friend, and tend to be candid accounts of a combination of the reviewer's actual and perceived experience.

The empty shelf and the rude behavior get posted on-line and that becomes your reputation. Try to fight that with a stick.

I find this very exciting! I see it as yet one more opportunity to show "There is Power in the Clarity of Your Articulation."

Think of it this way: When you learn to harness your word choice, you gain control over your reputation. A review site on the Internet can give you a whole new place to shine. Making candid consumer review sites work to your benefit It requires vigilance; you have to be aware of how and what you communicate consistently. Fortunately, the purpose of this book is to teach you how to do just that. You have the potential to find yourself in control of the framework of your reputation, even on-line.

Play your cards right, and your spectacular communication skills could possibly attract customers to your door from further away than you had ever considered.

If you have a business in an area with a busy tourist trade, for example, it may be tempting to see the tourist who walks in as one person in a flood of people who will never be back again, who has no real influence in your community, who matters less than the locals who come in all the time. Why hold a conversation, make extra effort, or even make eye contact? Another tourist will be along in a minute.

Let's rethink that for a moment. Tourists, in particular, like to post reviews on sites like Tripadvisor.com, a site offering an arena for both excited and weary travelers to share their experiences in each place they visited. They post personal and sometimes emotionally charged ratings of places where they ate, slept and shopped, as well as what activities they experienced on vacation, and how they were treated with each interaction. They do so because they know that other people who are

Exceptional Care for Your Valued Client

planning trips to the same spot will be jumping online to research what they want to see and do, and where they want to spend their money.

This practice is by no means limited to people traveling outside their usual spending zones, and it reminds us that every customer interaction, no matter how brief, demands our attention. Have you used a site like Yelp.com to help you find a florist or a dentist? This kind of web-site is popular with locals who refer to them specifically for insights about restaurants they have walked by a "million times," businesses with confusing names, self-proclaimed "experts" on anything from dog grooming to plumbing, and tiny hole-in-the-wall stores that could be hiding trash or treasure.

Essentially, going to a website for information is akin to getting a recommendation from a friend; online reviews from amateurs who write outside the professional arena of the critic or work outside the industry they're writing about are deemed to be unbiased and therefore easier to trust.

So how do you create and keep the "good customers" who return to do business with you and/or bring other customers to your door? Maybe it will help if we change our word choice from "good customer" to "happy customer." You will see it immediately eliminates a number of the attributes listed above.

- A happy customer comes back time and time again.
- A happy customer brings other customers to your door.
- A happy customer asks questions.
- A happy customer makes conversation, even if it's just small talk.
- A happy customer points out a problem, trusting you to create a solution.
- A happy customer pays on time.

In a nutshell, a happy customer is one who believes they have forged a bond or some sort of connection with you. A little bit goes a long way

Section 1

to building this connection; a warm greeting and a smile of recognition can instantly create the belief in your customer: "I'm welcome here."

The customer with a problem or concern will do one of two things. He will suffer in silence and then broadcast the news in public, when and where it's too late for you to do anything about it. Or, he will call you on it; give you the opportunity to explain, apologize, solve or repair the situation, and then go out and broadcast the news in public.

When it comes to your Exceptional Care paradigm, the way you incorporate communication will dictate what this customer says to you, and then what he or she says to everyone else. The customer who suffered silently will outline and focus on the details of the problem. The customer who brings the issue to your attention will still outline the problem, and then he will also outline what you did about it. If the results were pleasing, the review will be glowing. Which would you prefer?

Fortunately, you already have all the tools you need to help your customers associate *your* business with where they feel most comfortable and confident conducting *their* business. It is just a matter of learning what the most effective tools are, what they're for, why they're important, and how to use them. The fun part comes with the fact that each of your employees has them, too. They bring these tools to work with them every day. They just need the insight and then the permission to use them the right way.

Imagine what you can build together once you have taught them what you learn here!

When you focus on creating happy customers, you get rewarded with good customers. **"Exceptional Care for Your Valued Client"** says it all. Take care of them, and they will take care of you.

Challenges within the greater economy make it absolutely essential to address and adjust what you're doing to serve your existing clients. Success depends first and foremost on how you communicate with them and what you do to make them want to bring their friends and family into contact with you. Create a strong fan base within the customer

Exceptional Care for Your Valued Client

group you already have and the other potential customers out there that you want to attract will come along virtually on their own.

Every once in a while, we will be using the term **Exceptional Care** throughout the book to help you begin to reframe the old paradigm of Customer Service. The new paradigm stands on the shoulders of the old, reaching above and beyond your client's expectations in order to provide Exceptional Care.

Create Signature Moments for your customers. Be memorable. Provide **Exceptional Care for Your Valued Client!**

Section 1

Chapter 2

There is Power in the Clarity of Your Articulation™

Even if you consider yourself an expert in the field of **Exceptional Care**, there is always room for improvement.

By its very nature, business needs to keep up in order to stay afloat; and in order to thrive, you have to stay ahead. Looking for the next super cool marketing tool or flashy advertising campaign is a common practice. Others invest in the most expensive cutting-edge technology or production software; while searching for the next hottest "thing" so they can jump on the bandwagon and ride it till the wheels fall off – all before their customers do.

What if I told you the secret behind success in business has more to do with old-fashioned practices than latest-gadget applications?

Once you get past all the hype about the latest on-line social networking craze, the "speed of business," and all the fantastic technology out there that helps you connect instantly with your customers and keep your business uppermost in their minds, you must remember that it is your word choice in each and every one of these spheres that will make or break all of your efforts.

Human beings respond well to good communication, and respond poorly to bad communication. If you employ good communication skills in your business, your customers will respond well to you. The opposite is also true. What you need to know and understand is that there is no equality in this equation. Customers respond far more aggressively to poor communication skills than to good ones.

People share good customer experiences with a handful of friends. We expect to be treated well where and when we spend our money. We may notice a pleasant interchange, but do we shout it from the rooftops like we do when we are mistreated? No.

Exceptional Care for Your Valued Client

Poor communication skills can cost you your business. As I've said before, all those human beings running around from one business to another in the course of their daily lives have an enormous amount of power literally at their fingertips. Have you heard of Twitter? A disgruntled customer can upload a complaint to the Internet from his smart phone before he has left your store. And in a few minutes, hundreds and in some cases thousands of people know about how terrible their customer experience was; and how bad your employee's "customer service" is!

Here is a sobering statistic: According to the White House Office of Consumer Affairs, the average person remembers a bad customer service experience for 23.5 years, and they spend the first 18 months telling everyone they know all about it. Can you imagine 18 months of someone bad-mouthing you, your company or your product on the Internet, using a social networking tool like Facebook or Yelp to tell the story over and over and over? *Source: Cynthia Messer, 2004, At Your Service: Working with Multicultural Customers*

There are countless reasons to avoid the embarrassment of having a reputation for bad customer service. Okay, you caught me; there's really just one: So you can stay in business.

It is nowhere near enough to simply avoid a bad reputation. Building a good reputation is a step in the right direction. To be successful, you must understand the importance of intentionally creating positive and effective customer service experiences. There's that **Exceptional Care for Your Valued Client** idea again.

The foundation of everything I teach, whether in a workshop, a newsletter, an article, a one-on-one coaching session, or a corporate consultation, is this: "There is Power in the Clarity of Your Articulation." I would like to invite you to think about that for a minute.

There is Power in the Clarity of Your Articulation.

This phrase translates into far more than simply speaking clearly, but that's where we're going to start.

Section 1

Adapting the catchphrase to customer service situations, you could rewrite it thus: *There is Exceptional Care for Your Valued Client in the Clarity of Your Articulation.*

That's a mouthful!

Think about it. If you are able to identify *Exceptional Care for Your Valued Client* as your "power," you will see it makes sense, and that it does actually require clarity in your articulation. Once you master that skill, providing a high level of customer service will follow quite naturally.

As with Signature Moments, I will break this down for you throughout the book, and you will see the power and potential in that one phrase, and, I hope, become just as excited about it as I am.

To introduce the idea, I encourage you to ruminate on it this way: When you communicate clearly with your clients, you provide them with Exceptional Care. And that's what brings them coming back for more.

Again, it sounds simple, however learning the art of clear and congruent communication can be tricky, and requires you be vigilant about what you say and how you say it – every time you open your mouth, put up a sign, make a chart, create an ad, or craft any kind of message for your customers.

As you will learn through the process of reading this book and applying the lessons to your own diction and behavior, clarity is linked to respect, which in turn is linked to listening skills, body language, building a Framework of Rapport, being sympathetic to multiple points of view without losing your own, and being able to articulate intentions, expectations and solutions – all of which bring you right back to the importance of clarity.

Learning to identify, own and use strong communication skills is a truly empowering process. As I take you through the fascinating experience of consciously developing your own personal communication skills as well as the skills of those around you, you will be amazed by the shifts

Exceptional Care for Your Valued Client

in your existing paradigms, even the small ones, and the big results that come from them. The kind of care and attention you give your clients is defined by your communication skills, enhanced by it, and falls apart without it.

Regardless of the size of your business, whether you are face-to-face with customers every day, or you have an army of employees who do that for you, the need to perfect your communication skills must be your priority.

For simplicity's sake, from here on let's assume that "you" and "your" are umbrella statements that include you personally, as well as each person throughout your business entrusted with any form of customer service interaction, from the entry-level employee on up to the CEO, or whatever title translates into "the buck stops here."

Today, like never before, word of mouth can make you or break you. Remember, people react to how they believe they are being treated, and if it's less than what they think they deserve, they will tell everyone they know. Technology has expanded the typical list of "everyone they know" to include hundreds and sometimes thousands of people. And it only takes moments to post an opinion online.

The upside of all this is that really good communication skills can save your bacon. In their weakest application, which is still strong, they can prevent misunderstandings. In their strongest application, good communication skills can forge relationships and bonds between business and customer that stretch across many years – sometimes generations – and endure many changes and challenges.

Every single person in your company who comes in contact with a customer, whether in person, on the phone, or over the Internet, will only ever deliver an Exceptional Care experience equal to his or her communication skills.

That bears repeating.

Section 1

Every single person in your company who comes in contact with a customer will only ever deliver an Exceptional Care experience equal to his or her communication skills.

Doubt it? Consider this scenario:

Two people are assigned the task of answering phones in the same call center. They are expected to answer the phone with the same greeting and ask for the same information to open the call. It has been established that customers call the service line with any combination of the same 15 to 18 questions or issues that can be answered or resolved in one conversation. The questions are so common and so predictable that the two new-hires are each given a standard script from which to read. The script even provides a selection of two or three pleasant and professional ways to close the call.

One of the new hires takes genuine interest in providing solutions for the customers who call the help line. She takes pleasure in giving them the answers they need to successfully go about their business, and answers the phone with a smile and attitude of expectancy; she expects to be able to help.

Because she has this attitude, she listens carefully to each question and happily turns to the page in her script that walks her through solving that specific problem. She might even make mall talk during necessary lulls in the conversation to reassure the customer that she is still on the line and engaged in the solution process.

When a question comes up that is outside the limits of the script and her experience, she asks the customer if he minds being put on hold so she can transfer him to someone who can address his unique concerns, and does it in such a way that instead of feeling shunted around from one person to another, he feels like he is getting special treatment.

Her communication skills, or the way she combines speaking, listening, and responding, have made the customer feel unique, special and satisfied that he got to work with a human being to resolve his issue.

Exceptional Care for Your Valued Client

The other new hire is in it for the paycheck. He has no idea how his tone and attitude translate to the person on the other line. After all, he's just repeating words in a script. He's human, therefore, by default, when he answers the phone he's giving the customer a human being to talk to, right?

This new-hire fails to connect with the individuals on the other end of the line, so they hold no interest for him. He quickly becomes impatient with the same stupid questions over and over. He can tell from reading the script that every one of those questions has an obvious answer, so how dumb do you have to be to call and ask anyway?

He is unable to relate to the customer's confusion, let alone distress. Listening is a waste of time, and saying anything more than what's been written down for him in the script is a waste of breath. In fact, he has shortened some of the answers to get rid of what he thinks are unnecessary steps.

There are some parts of the script he has to say verbatim, namely the greeting and whichever of the closing remarks he picks. He says them so much and cares so little about them that he fails to hear himself speak when he does.

From the greeting on through the rest of the call he repeats the script as fast as possible, gets annoyed when asked to slow down or repeat himself, and lets his mind wander as he plays with the stress ball on his desk. His mind is already on the next call and his finger is already moving to disconnect this one. He manages to make the carefully crafted closing remark sound like a dismissal.

How many times have you felt like an interruption or an intruder when you were a customer? On the phone or in person? How did you feel about the company you were trying to deal with? One bad apple really does spoil the barrel.

This example demonstrates one of my fundamental beliefs, and a concept I will elaborate on later, which is the importance of the role

Section 1

congruency plays in successful communication. More importantly, it helps me make the point that society's indicators of mental acuity – namely IQ, vocabulary, "book smarts," and level of formal education achieved – have little to do with effective communication. If you can stop your mouth for just a minute, you can replace what's about to come out of it. My strategies are very simple, and anyone can use them.

Does it matter which of the new hires in the story has the more extensive vocabulary? No. As long as you choose words with clear meanings and deliver them in congruence with the other elements of communication – namely respect, body language, attentiveness, listening skills, something I call respond-ability, and empathy for another's perspective – you have all the power you need to deliver exceptional care for your valued client.

Anyone can learn these techniques and benefit from their application. The only limitation lies in your willingness to practice them effectively, embrace the changes you will have to make, and enjoy the results. That is why it is imperative that you read this book, absorb the information, use the tools with vigilance and share them, even if only by demonstration, with everyone in your business.

Each and every person from the entry-level employee to the CEO can use these tools effectively. What we teach within these pages is based on what you already have at your fingertips. Regardless of the scope of your vocabulary, through careful and considerate word choice you can begin elevating your customer service and client communication skills today.

After all, regardless of the nature of your business, you are in it to attract and maintain customers. You may think you're in it to make money. That is actually a bit misleading. Your purpose for being in business is to *find and keep your clients*. Money is the happy result of *having those clients*. The more customers you have, the more money will come with them. If the customers stop, the money stops. Therefore, invest in your business by investing in your relationships with your customers.

It is a mistake to see your customer as a tool to get you to some other

Exceptional Care for Your Valued Client

goal, like a quota, bottom line, or expansion. It is a mistake to allow your employees to believe the customer is either a necessary speed bump on the road to a paycheck, or just a way to kill time until the shift ends – let alone an unwelcome interruption. AND the biggest mistake is the failure to recognize when and why this is happening.

If it happens occasionally or even most of the time, then it is a bad habit and you can do something about it. Every now and then the problem's origin is deeper than habit; you simply have the wrong person in the job. We will talk about that later, too. Part of providing "Exceptional Care for Your Valued Client" is being able to place the best communicators in front of the customer, identifying those who would do better behind the scenes, and moving them there.

If you find yourself wondering why you seem to have lost some customers, or why your business fails to bring the people "out there" "in here," or your customer numbers are stable but the turn-over of faces is high, chances are somewhere along the line you forgot those numbers represent individual human beings, and you need to connect with them on the human level so they know you are willing and able to fulfill their needs and desires. You need to relearn how to communicate with them.

Every business has its core group of customers, its bread-and-butter set. They are the daily "16oz latte;" the monthly "single-pallet shipment;" the quarterly "figure out my sales taxes;" or the annual "company retreat." Regardless of other fluctuations in your business, regardless of seasons and trends, changes in holiday spending, or reactions to up- and down-swings in the market, whatever bits and pieces these customers bring to you is your constant, your minimum business that keeps you in business. You count on them for baseline productivity and will hardly get rich from their business alone, yet what would your business look like if you lost them?

So the challenge becomes managing relationships with your existing customers even as you reach out to embrace new ones. And you guessed it: Clear communication is your solution.

Section 1

There are many parts of communication; many layers, factors, aspects, attributes – whatever you want to call them, there are many pieces needing to fit together and work together in order to elevate your Exceptional Care skills and produce the results you are after. If you want to create Signature Moments that keep your customers coming back for more, aim beyond proficiency and tweak the details with your personal flair to take it to the next level.

Exceptional Care for Your Valued Client

Section 1

Chapter 3

Remember the Ice and Untie Your (K)nots

It's time to have some fun. In the upcoming pages I will cheerfully attack the foundation of your vocabulary, knock it down and help you rebuild it. There is so much power in these pages; it's probably going to blow your mind. It is my favorite part, and it's where the principles of "Remember the Ice and Other Paradigm Shifts" first come into play.

And play is what we're going to do. We're going to play with word choice and take a stab at sharpening those communication skills. The exercises throughout the book are important, so pay attention; they're going to show you just how confusing we can be with our messages to customers, and what we need to do about it.

The first word we're going to tackle is the worst offender. "Not" is the Beelzebub of the human vocabulary. Boy and how this over-used, annoying little trickster befuddles us and works its mischief! It ties our sentences into knots, which is why, throughout this book, you will find "Not" written as (k)not.

I do this to remind you that a *not* is, essentially, a *knot*. (K)nots tie up, delay and muddle communication. It's a new way to look at the phrase "tongue-tied." Why would you place a (k)not in an otherwise clear sentence? It's like making a noose to choke the life out of your message. And the worst part is; you're tying it up yourself!

I have been passionate about word choice since I was about 12 years old. I've been a student and teacher, observer and practitioner in one form or another for all of the years that have followed. I have been turning over and tweaking these concepts for decades, applying each to as many situations and relationships as have come my way.

The story behind "Remember the Ice" comes from an opportunity I had years ago to show a friend what a simple change in word choice could

Exceptional Care for Your Valued Client

do for his business. It is a story that has inspired countless testimonials from people who have adapted it to improve their own lives.

"In a convenience store on Northern Avenue in Phoenix, Arizona, the manager, Rick, had placed a couple of signs above his cash registers. His intention was to encourage his patrons to buy more ice during the hot desert summer.

I lived across the street from this store and came to know him fairly well. One day when I stepped up to the counter to make a purchase, I glanced again at the two signs above his cash registers that read "DON'T FORGET THE ICE" and decided to ask him how his ice sales were going.

You may think this was a strange question, but I have always been intrigued by the juxtaposition of words. I am also intrigued by the outcomes of behavior and how the two are intertwined.

Rick replied that ice sales were slow; he was unable to move his inventory with any speed or consistency, and most of it just sat there. We were in Phoenix, in the desert, in the middle of summer where it was 110 degrees in the shade on a cool day.

"Can I make a suggestion?" I asked. "Do you have a couple of pieces of paper and a Magic Marker I could use?" He gave me the items and I quickly made two new signs for him to place above his cash registers instead. The new signs read:

"REMEMBER THE ICE!!!"

I left with a knowing smile and purposely stayed away for about three weeks. When I did go back to the store, I spoke with Rick about his recent ice sales.

He was having difficulty keeping up with demand.

"I have had to triple my order in the last three weeks," he said. "Sales are great."

Section 1

I smiled and explained what I had done. "If I say to you," I began, "'Don't think of the color blue,' what color do you immediately think of?"

"Why, blue of course," he replied.

"Of course," I grinned. "Now, if I say 'Don't Forget the Ice', what will you forget?"

"Hmm ... the ice!"

"Right."

With a simple shift in word choice, Rick noticed a considerable increase in his ice sales. He shared the following with me:

"Bob, as the customers stand at the counter to check out, they look up, see the new sign – 'Remember the Ice' – and usually say, 'By the way, add a couple of bags of ice as well.' They pay for their items, pick up their ice from the freezer outside the door, and go on their way."

(Side note: His ice sales increased over 500% in the first 30 days after I changed the sign!)

Changing the imperative in those signs from "Don't Forget" to "Remember" changed the message from passive to active. How do you take the action to "(k)not" do something? There is no action in "(k)not" doing something, no direction to follow. If you want people to act, tell them what to do. If you want them to stop acting, to be still, tell them to "be still."

"Remember the ice" compelled Rick's customers to buy ice.

A simple change made a powerful impact. Improving your communication must begin with word choice because it is at the same time, both the logical beginning point and the most immediate and powerful change you can make.

Exceptional Care for Your Valued Client

So, let's begin.

All words have purpose. As we learn and grow, we develop a vocabulary of words we have harvested from the world around us. We learn to choose words that get us what we need. We learn to discard or refuse to use words that hurt others.

Sometimes, it takes a generation or two for a society to drop hurtful or incendiary words because common usage has entrenched them so deeply in automatic speech that there is a disconnect between saying it and accepting what is meant by saying it. It's just a word, right? It may no longer mean the same thing it used to, or carry the same weight, so why worry about using it? Shaking that word from your vocabulary is a process that involves awareness, substitution, reframing, and practice. Once you have taught yourself how to speak without a word, you lose the need to use it.

The first step toward owning this concept is to recognize that using the word is doing you a disservice.

I understand asking you to eliminate the word (k)not from your vocabulary is going to meet with resistance. Good! Resist it all you want. Challenge what I'm telling you. As long as you think it through, give it a go, and see what happens – that's all I ask.

I have witnessed so many powerful changes in the lives and businesses of my friends and clients across the country and around the world after implementing this first strategy, that I am confident once you start to play around with eliminating and replacing the (k)nots in your speech, you will start to realize how much more effective your communication has already become.

Common usage is an interesting phenomenon. Incorrect use of a word becomes accepted simply because an inordinate amount of people repeatedly and consistently make the error. It catches on, and pretty soon the error becomes commonplace, and we no longer notice there's anything wrong with what is being said.

Section 1

Did you know that *hopefully* is an adverb? It is used to describe an action. "Hailey stood at the window and watched hopefully for the dog to come back." She was hopeful. Hopefully describes how she watched. Today's common usage of the word "hopefully" is more like this:

"Hopefully, sales will spike in December."

"Hopefully, the customer will be patient."

Grammatically, neither makes sense. But we have become used to hearing and using "hopefully" this way, so much so that rarely does anyone notice it is incorrect. It no longer stands out as an odd way to use the word. We no longer notice it. Does that make it right? No. Just like the incorrect use of "hopefully," our brains no longer register what is wrong with the message when we use (k)nots.

Throwing a (k)not into a sentence for the sake of expediency or because it sounds like it belongs there is a similar phenomenon. In this next section we're going to look at some common customer service phrases that slip out automatically. I hear them with grating regularity. I'm going to use them to demonstrate how I hope your communication skills will evolve, and how easy it is to facilitate changes within your customer service messages that will elevate them to Exceptional Care messages.

The following are pretty standard "blow offs" that undermine the customer's need for information. I'm sure you can come up with more of your own to play with.

1. "He's not here."
2. "This guy's not happy."
3. "It's not ready."
4. "It's not going to be cheap."
5. "It's not a problem."
6. "It's not an easy thing to fix."
7. "She's not interested."

Exceptional Care for Your Valued Client

8. "That's not something we do."
9. "That's not my department."
10. "We're not able to see you today."

These statements are lazy, and they imply an unwillingness to take the customer's needs seriously. Worse, the first pass across the brain registers as the opposite of what is being said. Initially, "(k)not" fails to register. Regardless of how quickly the brain flips what is heard the first time to understand the message, a negative thought has made its impact. In the split nano-second of time it takes the brain to flip the (k)not and figure out the meaning of the sentence, the listener has a knee-jerk emotional reaction of frustration, annoyance, and confusion.

Take a look at the brain's first response to each of these statements, as well as the unspoken message that comes with it:

- "He's here" (but I'm sitting here at my desk, preventing you from seeing him). That is frustrating.
- "This guy's happy" (but the look on his face says otherwise). That is confusing.
- "It's ready" (but I'm preventing you from having it). Frustrating.
- "It's going to be cheap" (but then the bill says otherwise). Confusing.
- "It's a problem" (but I'm using a reassuring voice). Confusing.
- "It's an easy thing to fix" (but I'm making a big deal of this, charging a lot of money and telling you it's going to take a lot of time). Frustrating.
- "She's interested" (but she's refusing to accept the offer). Confusing.
- "That's something we do" (but for some reason I'm refusing to do it for you; I'm refusing to make the next move). Frustrating.
- "That's my department" (but I'm sitting here with a blank look on my face). Frustrating.
- "We're able to see you today" (but I'm withholding the opportunity from you). Frustrating.

Section 1

With a little effort, it's easy to reconstruct these sentences to avoid causing frustration and confusion.

1. "He's out of the office."
2. "This customer is unhappy."
3. "It is unfinished" or "It will be finished tomorrow."
4. "This is going to be expensive."
5. "I can do this easily."
6. "This is very challenging."
7. "She is no longer interested."
8. "We are unable to offer that."
9. "I am unable to do that."
10. "We are unable to fit you in today."

I believe with a touch more effort, you can do better.

He's not here" becomes an opportunity to inject a friendly, reassuring, and helpful tone.

"He's out of the office, and I expect he will return in an hour. Can I take a message, or can I help you?

"This guy's not happy" becomes: "This gentleman is frustrated. Could you please help me figure this out for him?"

"It's not ready" becomes: "There has been a delay, and the engineers are working on your project even as we speak."

"It's not going to be cheap" becomes: "We understand that this is an investment. If you have a minute I can walk you through all of the benefits that make this investment worthwhile."

"It's not a problem" becomes: "It's our pleasure. We enjoy providing this service for you. It is, after all, why we're in business."

Exceptional Care for Your Valued Client

"It's not an easy thing to fix" becomes: "This situation has presented a number of unique challenges. It will take time and attention to address it, but we are motivated to discover the best way to proceed in the most timely and cost-efficient manner."

"She's not interested" becomes: "You are very talented, however we showcase a different style here. Can I direct you to another agent who may be able to help you?"

"That's not something we do" becomes: ""We focus on getting your car back on the road after it's already here in the shop. Can I recommend a tow-truck company some of our other customers have used?"

"That's not my department" becomes: "Do you mind if I put you on hold for a moment, and then transfer you to Anthony Jones? He is trained to find a solution for you, and knows more about what we have to offer along those lines."

"We're not able to see you today" becomes: "I know you're anxious to see the dentist. Our next available appointment is at 11 a.m. on Friday. Would you like me to schedule that time for you, and allow me to call you if we have a cancellation between now and then?"

Part of the value in giving full answers that leave no room for (k)nots is you have to anticipate the customer's needs or next question in order to sound competent. When you demonstrate through full sentences you are giving the entire transaction considered thought, your customer will recognize he or she is important to you.

In this next part, I've included a few samples for you to play with on your own. Be sure to start with the simple removal of each (k)not so you increase your awareness of how the statement comes across before the brain registers it. It's important; skipping this step spoils the exercise.

"I'm not available."

Step 1: Remove the (k)not.
      "I'm available."

Section 1

Step 2: Replace the un-(k)not-ed or untied sentence with its opposite so that you get back to its original meaning.
"I'm unavailable."

Step 3: Rebuild the sentence with a different set of words.

"I'm busy right now."

Step 4: Rebuild the sentence with more information. Doing this allows the sentence to stand on its own; it can be removed from the context of the conversation and still deliver the news. "I'm busy for the next two hours. I will return phone calls at that time."

With your own business and specific customer service interactions in mind, take each of these sentences and move them through the four steps of communication evolution.

- "I'm not supposed to do this, but I will"
- "That is not how we do things"
- "That is not something we normally do"
- "This will not be available for you every time"
- "We're not the cheapest in town, but we are the best!"
- "This new item is not in the inventory yet"
- "We're not participating in that special offering"
- "That's not going to happen"
- "I'm not arguing with you"

As you can see, some of the worst mistakes in customer service come from an eagerness to help, yet backfire because of a distinct lack of finesse and a lack of understanding of the hidden message you're delivering. The temptation to tell a customer, "I'm not supposed to do this, but I will," may originate with the intention of letting them know you're willing to go above and beyond the norm for them, but it really just leaves your customer wondering what's wrong with your business that the service you're giving them is such a big deal.

For example, you may ship 1800 boxes of bobble-head dolls to Sri Lanka 18 times a week, yet you must treat your customer as though she were

Exceptional Care for Your Valued Client

the only person on the planet shipping anything anywhere, and that you opened your doors that day just for her. Your job is to remember that she has no interest in how many times you repeat shipping prices and timelines to your customers, let alone how bored you are when you have to go over it all again. All she cares about is the one time you quote it to her.

Conversely, she must be made to feel the exact same way when her needs strain your abilities. Indicating that sending packages to Sri Lanka is a logistical nightmare but you'll "do it anyway" will earn you no additional respect. In fact, you run the risk of losing respect in her eyes. Have you ever had the feeling that your business was an imposition to the person helping you?

If you have been in business for five minutes you can anticipate at least a few of your customers' concerns and questions. Be ready to offer information without having to be begged, prodded or cajoled for it. Customers rarely enjoy feeling like they're trying to get blood from a stone when all they want to know is they can trust you to take care of them.

As you develop the habit of thinking before you speak, you will begin to create full, meaningful messages without having to pause for any mental gymnastics. Although a quick, clear phrase from Step 2 or Step 3 may seem like the expedient way to go, and are adequate fall-backs when you're extremely busy, your client is entitled to explanations that address his or her concerns.

Of course, this means you must be knowledgeable, empowered to make decisions, and trained in the appropriate way to share information. That combination enables you to think on your feet and satisfy the customer even in the most uncomfortable confrontations. While solid communication skills are designed to prevent confrontations, they tend to be inevitable, especially when your customer has emotions at stake. Make an effort when you communicate. There are a number of simple ways to rephrase these remarks to get you to Step 2, and I encourage you to rely on them as you begin to practice substituting other words for those (k)nots.

Section 1

The end goal is to eliminate (k)nots from your vocabulary, and it's okay to take your time getting used to it. Re-learning how to speak is a process that we will spell out for you later. In the meantime, remember practice will make your responses more comfortable and more easily dispersed. Eventually, however, I want you to begin to think on your feet, and create the full sentences that will become the power tools in your exceptional care kit.

At first, pausing to rebuild your message will feel awkward, so you may find you lean heavily on Step 2 for a while. Very quickly, I assure you, you will begin to challenge yourself to go beyond simple rephrasing, and you will find yourself choosing the best and most powerful messages from a selection that springs to mind. In my experience, most people find Steps 3 and 4 exhilarating. It is a unique, empowering process which builds confidence and feels good to do.

One of the most empowering side-effects of untying (k)nots from your language is that you have to stop yourself from speaking, at least for a moment, in order to prevent yourself from tying your messages up with (k)nots in the first place. Can you imagine how different your day would be if each person you talked to were to stop talking long enough to weigh what they were going to say next?

The problem with (k)not is in its purpose. It is intended to invert your sentence to mean the opposite of what you're saying. And the purpose is disempowering. It is a negative word attached to disappointment, mistakes, reprimands, and confusion, and the worst part is that it is so subtle we rarely attribute our confusion and annoyance specifically to it. To top it off, we use it so much and rely on it so heavily that our brains no longer register its meaning.

(K)not is an insidious little word that stands in the way of clear and effective communication.

Your customer is wondering if he can buy something at your store on Sunday. Will you be open or closed?

Exceptional Care for Your Valued Client

Here is what happens when you say "We're not open on Sundays":

As we pointed out before, your customer's brain registers "Open Sundays." Then it goes through a process of double-checking that fact because something about it seems wrong. It responds to the cue from (k)not to search for the opposite of "open," which is "closed." It then reforms the sentence to get the right meaning. It may happen in a split second, but it happens, and it's a waste of effort, no matter how small.

Chances are, your customer will habitually forget whether you are open on Sundays, and, worst case scenario, will find a store with a less confusing schedule. It's an interesting phenomenon that happens with stunning consistency.

But wait. That's hardly a confusing schedule, right? What's this guy's problem? His problem is that you failed to answer an easy question with an easy answer. You created a problem because you tied your message up with a (k)not. You missed the opportunity to be clear and memorable: "We are closed on Sundays"

Here is what happens when you say, "We are closed on Sundays": Your customer's brain registers "Closed Sundays." And that's it. Message received. Your customer will develop the habit of making a conscious effort to include you in Saturday or weekday plans because he will always know, with complete confidence. You are closed on Sundays.

I have been using very basic examples to illustrate my point. Think of all the times in a given day when you are confronted with multiple (k)nots in a single sentence or paragraph. Sometimes it gets so bad we do become aware of the mental gymnastics our brains are performing to figure out what a sentence really means.

"If he hadn't done that he wouldn't have ended up with results he didn't realize weren't the ones he didn't want all along." My brain hurts just coming up with that one!

You must become alert to the fact that even the tiniest (k)nots have the potential to undermine you, your message, and your business. The next

Section 1

chapter is devoted to exploring how (k)not in combination with other words "kills its host."

We use (k)nots too much because we are lazy. They slip in automatically without our thought, awareness, or intention. They make us lazy in our speech, and then in our messaging by turn. The irony is this lazy inclination that actually creates more work for both parties. It seems so much easier to use a (k)not than to construct a straightforward sentence, however it confuses the people we're talking to, over-complicates the simple beauty of clear communication, and leads to very frustrating exchanges.

It is actually far simpler to say what you mean the first time, clearly and concisely. Often it's a case of having to relearn how to speak in order to realize that. Tying a (k)not into what we're saying is so deeply ingrained in our patterns of speech that for most people it will take some effort to go through the steps to break that (k)notty habit. Once you replace the (k)notty habit with good, clear, communication habits you will find that it's far easier and more empowering to live without.

Poor word choice can make the most well-meaning among us come across in the worst ways. If you could get all of your company's customer service interactions to be clear and consistent across the board, what would your daily business reality look like? If your customer service team became an Exceptional Care team, what kinds of results can you imagine? If I told you it can begin to happen immediately, as soon as you drop that (k)not from every customer service interaction, how soon would you do it?

The sooner you learn to eliminate (k)not from your vocabulary, the sooner you will be able to reap the rewards of clear communication. That learning process is what I'm going to take you through in this book. I believe if you are fully aware of what you are doing and how to recognize the stages you are going through as you relearn your communication skills, you will enjoy the process and share it with others more readily.

Exceptional Care for Your Valued Client

I'm betting you're pretty skeptical. Good. Doubt me, fight me, and refuse to believe us. We are asking you to do it anyway. The why and the how are in these chapters, *and* the practical application is in your hands, or rather, on the tip of your tongue.

Section 1

Chapter 4

The Pitfalls of Tying "Do" Up In (K)nots

Think about this: Most people in business, from customer service representatives up through the highest levels of management, have given in to the idea they must allocate a certain percentage of their time to clearing up misunderstandings by explaining or clarifying information that is already in writing or has already been said.

Customer headaches – or rather, the headaches you get from dealing with confused and irritated customers – are a big part of your day, right? That is why so many companies have entire departments and training manuals devoted to resolving customer issues. How many of these issues do you think you could avoid by taking an entirely new, yet almost absurdly simple, proactive approach to communicating with your customers?

What if you had a magic wand that could somehow make each and every one of your messages clear and concise? Would eliminating those headaches and the time they steal from your day make a difference to your productivity, your ability to achieve goals, your peace of mind or enjoyment at work? To be able to take back that time and redirect that energy would truly be empowering. When you are able to craft what you are going to say with confidence, knowing it is clear and valid, you will find renewed inspiration within your language choices.

How empowering do you think it would be to know your words influence and inspire, rather than confuse and annoy? I believe few people actually set out to confuse and annoy others. I believe most of us want to be clear and make sense. I believe most people just need to know how to do it.

The good news is you already have everything you need at your disposal. Without getting up from your chair or purchasing accessories, you can begin to make positive changes in the way you handle customer service situations. It's just a matter of understanding the how and why of

Exceptional Care for Your Valued Client

organizing and using your words, and putting it all into practice. The first hurdle is recognizing poor word choice for what it is, and how disempowering and counterproductive it can be.

In a customer service situation, poor word choice undermines and diminishes your company's image, reputation and competitive edge. In other words: It undermines and diminishes your power. Once you own this fact, you can begin the process of selecting the most common offenders and usurping their roles in your life with better words.

Do we really need to get rid of the word (k)not? Yes. In fact, I eliminated it from my vocabulary decades ago (I even cut it out of my dictionary). Ever since I did that, I have experienced some very powerful results that continue to have an impact on my personal life as well as my professional career. So what's the big deal, anyway? Simple: The issue with (k)not is that when we use it we indicate that we mean the opposite of what we have just said. It is important to note that this also applies to conjugated words where "not" turns into "n't", as with "do not" and "don't". In order to slip a (k)not into a sentence, we have to invert the message of the sentence to indicate its opposite. We are better served when we construct the sentence to say what we mean in the first place.

Let's go back to the story behind "Remember the Ice," when I first outlined the dilemmas created by the word "don't." This is a fun place to start expanding from the basic (k)not to the other (k)notty words that have ingratiated themselves into our common usage.

The first word choice game, or exercise, I am going to invite you to play is simple and can be pretty entertaining, depending on how you spend your time.

Tell yourself to be aware each time the words "don't forget" pop up in the next 24 hours. When they do, replace them with "remember." and reconstruct the sentence.

Here are a few examples:

Section 1

- Don't forget to mention the special promotion
- Don't forget to be on time
- Don't forget to smile
- Don't forget to call him back
- Don't forget to give each person a receipt

When you talk to yourself and you're tempted to use a "don't," take a breath and choose to phrase it differently. Instead of "Don't forget to take a sweater" stop yourself and say, "Remember to take a sweater." See what happens.

After reading the "Remember the Ice" story, a woman who was constantly forgetting where she put her keys decided to do something different. Instead of reciting, "Don't forget the keys," she began to say to herself "Remember the keys" and "Remember the keys are on this counter," as she placed them there. And she would indeed remember the keys – and where she had put them.

She practiced this conscious process consistently until it became an almost unconscious habit. A year later, she has found that she can tell herself to remember anything throughout her day, go about her business without any anxiety, and her mind will do as it is told without fail.

If she gets a call at work first thing in the morning to run an errand at the end of the day, she can rely on herself to remember to follow through; the instructions she gave herself will come to the forefront of her mind when it needs to. The task or item pops into her head at the perfect time, every time. She is able to trust the power of a clear statement because she knows it works.

Here are some more small changes that have the potential to make a big difference in our every day lives.

"Don't forget to buy cat food" – Lara would buy everything else in the store, but forget the cat food, until she started saying "Remember to buy cat food."

Exceptional Care for Your Valued Client

"Don't forget the cell phone charger" – Max would leave chargers in hotel rooms across the country. Thinking and saying "Remember the cell phone charger" as he plugs it in, almost guarantees he will remember it, and pack it in his bag before checking it out.

"Don't forget to grab the thumb drive with the presentation from Jim's computer" – Alex would like to forget the flap he caused when he forgot the thumb drive. "Remember to grab the disc with the presentation from Jim's computer" is a clear instruction that inspires action. When Alex goes through the mental checklist of what to bring to a presentation, it includes only that which he has told himself to remember.

"Don't forget to sign Sarah up for soccer this afternoon." – Jeanne would like to forget Sarah's face when she had to tell her daughter she had forgotten to do it. Now Jeanne remembers to follow through on what is important to Sarah by saying things like "Remember to sign Sarah up for soccer this afternoon."

"Well, this sounds like a neat parlor trick," you may be thinking. "But what does it have to do with customer service, let alone providing exceptional care?"

As I showed you in the "Remember the Ice" story, when you use "don't" in your direct instructions to a customer you set them up to fail; you set them up to be unable to fulfill your request.

I'll show you what I mean: Rick intended to ask his customers to buy ice. That, essentially, is what you are doing when you communicate with a customer; you are asking him to take an action, specifically to buy a product or service from you. Yet the words Rick chose in his original signsmade it difficult for his customers to oblige. He chose the verb "to forget," so what he was telling them to do was to "forget" to buy ice. The effective verb choice would have been "to remember," and as I demonstrated, as soon as he asked his customers to remember, they did. They fulfilled his request over the next 30 days to the tune of five times his normal ice sales.

Section 1

The best way to get results from your customers is to ask them clearly and specifically, and respectfully, to do what you want. Why clutter the request with ineffective language? Of course, the greatest success comes from listening to them. I'll go into that more in future chapters.

The purpose of this book is to share both the techniques I have developed over the years and the logic behind each of them. If it seems like I'm repeating myself or drilling these concepts into your head over and over, it's because I am. You have had your entire life to develop "(k)notty word" habits. The first step to breaking those habits is to become fully conscious of them. The more I bring them to your attention, and the more obvious I make them, the more you will notice your use of them and the sooner you will be able to develop new, more empowering habits.

My task is to keep working on your conscious processes and your level of awareness until the changes I encourage become automatic. Repetition is the mother of skill, so I repeat, repeat, repeat in order to help you develop this skill. When you strengthen your communication skills then turn around and apply them to customer service, you end up providing exceptional care for your valued clients almost by default. And that is how you strengthen your business – in any economy.

I am constantly amazed by how the simple solutions I put forward have such tremendous results. You would think that by now it would be commonplace to me, but I am delighted every time. I expect changes in word choice to have a certain degree of effectiveness, however, the ripple effect can be staggering in its reach. It is tremendously exciting to watch my clients reap the expected and the unexpected, and to experience the increase in skill and confidence that automatically follows.

Let me share an ongoing, powerful, Remember the Ice success story from my web-site, www.remembertheice.com. In October 2008, I met Cornelis de Maijer from Hoogland, The Netherlands. He is the managing partner for a luxury sailing yacht company catering to those desiring a posh and pampered cruise on the Mediterranean Sea.

Exceptional Care for Your Valued Client

"You really experience *Absolute Freedom*", explains Cornelis.

Our connection was fostered through www.Ecademy.com, a popular social and business networking web-site. Cornelis used the search mechanism to find a fellow member with a background in "Positive Word Choice." Lo and behold, I was his direct match.

In a Skype conversation a few days after first reading my profile, Cornelis said, "Bob, Remember the Ice is such a simple, yet powerful concept to help me with my word choice. In my previous content on my website, I had some poisonous words," he said. "I was using (k)notty words in my content."

Specifically, he had had this statement up on his site for a very long time:

"Don't forget to book early."

One simple sentence with a misguided message had a profound impact on his bookings through the years. He was gaining a modest 12-15% increase in bookings for his sailing yachts off the Turkish coast. The same disempowering words were on his brochure as well.

After being introduced to Remember the Ice he changed his wording to:

Remember to book early, and experience the difference!

That summer was Cornelis' 14th season in the sailing yacht business, and it became his most productive. By the middle of July his bookings had topped 165%, and he had already secured 20 bookings for the following year.

On a recent Skype call, Cornelis shared, "Bob, booking for the next year in advance is something new for us – and I like it very much! Being in the seasonal leisure and tourism business, advanced bookings for the next season, the next year, is very special, and as far as I understand from my colleagues, they have to put forth a lot of effort in gaining 'repeat' or early bookings by their clients."

The exciting part is how fast Cornelis experienced results. There are two areas where he made changes and had success.

Section 1

- He changed the "(k)notty words" from "Don't forget" to "Remember to book early".

- He embraced the concept of eradicating the "(k)notty words" in his written and spoken conversations on a daily basis. He got involved with the program, and made changes.

The best part is, he continues to be excited about using **Remember the Ice**, and his wife and children are catching on as well. Cornelis is a continuing success story.

If you can take this in on a nuts-and-bolts level, you will move quickly from untying (k)nots as you're speaking, to constructing sentences that stand on their own. Great change can indeed begin this small. Remember though, it is the practice that cements the change.

Now that you have made the decision to test this theory; untie your (k)nots, and see what a difference it can make in your customer service interactions as you develop exceptional care. I encourage you to challenge yourself to stay alert and to increase your focus to the point of being hyper-aware of the words you use. Challenge yourself to maintain a higher level of awareness as you listen to others and observe language usage in the world around you, especially in marketing campaigns and customer service interactions.

(K)not is more than a *"chaos causer"*; it is a leech. Think of all the other words it attaches itself to in our everyday speech, sucking out the functional meaning of the word and inverting the meaning to subvert its power. I have identified a group of the most frequent offenders that I call "Not and the Hit List Six":

- Not
- Don't (do not)
- Can't (cannot)
- Couldn't (could not)
- Won't (will not)

Exceptional Care for Your Valued Client

- Wouldn't (would not)
- Shouldn't (should not)

We have already taken a look at "don't" in everyday situations. Now let's examine why it's important to replace it with something more constructive when you're interacting with customers.

Often, when you use the word "don't" in a business location, for example, you do so to prevent your customer from taking an undesirable action. However, most of the time you're simply planting the seed of that behavior in their head when you tell them (k)not to do something. Is there anything more annoying than having to repeat yourself and/or a printed sign

- "Don't touch the display case" registers as "Touch the display case."
- "Don't walk on the grass" registers as "walk on the grass."
- "Don't leave your empty cartons here" registers as "Leave your empty cartons here." There's that
- "Don't think of the color blue" concept all over again.

You just put the idea into your customer's head to touch your display case, walk on the grass, and leave his empty cartons behind.

One of the basic lessons in clear communication is how to give clear instructions. That means that it's up to you to provide the active alternative to the action you want to prevent your customers from taking. Empower them to make the right choice.

- "Please ask an employee to open the display case"
- "Please stay on the path"
- "Please place your empty containers in this box"

Remember that "don't" breaks down to "do not." Do is an action verb, as in "do this" and "do that." Elementary, right? Why am I spelling out something so simple? Am I being condescending? No. I am reminding

Section 1

you of something that is indeed elementary, so elementary I bet you no longer give any thought to it so that you will begin to respect even the tiny, commonplace words that come out of your mouth.

Do you give thought to flicking your eyes to the rear view mirror when you're driving, or is it an automatic action? Do you say to yourself, "Turn the key to the left" when you unlock your front door at night, or is it an automatic turn of the wrist that takes no thought at all? You had to practice each action to make it automatic. At some point I'd wager you had to remind yourself that turning the key to the right was the wrong way - or that turning it to the left was the right way - to unlock the door. Simple instructions are just as important to practice as the more complex ones. I would say they are more important because the simple instructions are the building blocks for the complex ones.

When you say "don't," you are saying, "do not." When you say, "do not," you are saying "take the action: not." You may argue that "don't touch the display case" and "don't walk on the grass" imply keeping your hands to yourself and walking on the path. However, when you are dealing with clients and customers, leaving the correct action up to implication is nowhere near enough instruction to get them to do what you want. You must be clear enough so that even the most distracted and least cooperative of customers understands what's going on in your business and how they are to behave.

After all, instructions are about behavior. Which versions of the following instructions do you think is more comprehensive? Which invite more questions, worry, or confusion?

- "Don't forget to call us by 5 p.m."
- "Remember to call us before 5 p.m."

- "Don't forget to sign both sides of the page"
- "Remember to sign both sides of the page"

- "Don't leave your child unattended"
- "Please remain with your child at all times"

Exceptional Care for Your Valued Client

- "Don't worry about your dog"
- "Trust us to take care of your dog"

- "Don't wait here"
- "Please wait in the adjacent room"

Clear, concise instructions can be as brief as the lazy, tangled ones. Untying the (k)nots in your communication has the potential to streamline your business in ways that you may be unaware of.

Take Joe, for example, whose car repair shop is open from 8:00 a.m. to 5:00 p.m. Experience has taught Joe that commuters in his area need to be on buses and trains before 8:00 a.m., and that a lot can happen to a car on the road after 6:00 p.m. So Joe has established a working solution to after-hours problems, and it is his new office manager's responsibility to explain how it works to anxious customers who have no idea how they're going to get their car in the shop without disrupting their work schedules.

Joe sits down to explain to Dana how it works. He is concerned about making sure she knows the process so she can help soothe those anxious customers, but he has yet to learn about excluding (k)nots from communication, and tends to believe that the more information he gives a customer, the more they will understand. Fortunately, Dana has some experience with the power of word choice and clarity.

"We can't let a customer think they can't get their car to us just because they can't be here when we open," He begins.

Dana picks up her pen, poised to take notes. It's already a little confusing.

"So what we do is; if they can't make it when we're open, we tell them it is okay to drop off their car over night. But, this is where it gets complicated. We're not open weekends so they can't park on the street Fridays because of the meters on Saturday. They can't park in the parking lot next door because that guy doesn't like it. Whatever you do, don't

Section 1

tell them to park next door because that guy will have a cow. Seriously, tell them they cannot park there, whatever they do." Joe is so concerned with where his customers "can't" park that he has neglected to tell her where they "can" park.

"What about the lot across the street?" Dana asks.

"Yeah, that's the only place they won't get a ticket or be towed." He indicates her notes, "Did you write that down? Just like that?"

Dana nods.

Joe continues, "Okay so we can't read minds. They need to write out who they are, what car is theirs, what's wrong with it, and how to reach them. We can't do any work until we talk to them. Ever. Remember that. We call those customers first thing. And we'll need their key. Can't do anything without a key. They can't forget to put the key and the note in an envelope with their name on it and put it in the mail slot in the front door. Do not let them put their key and envelope in that funky blue box thing out front because we won't get it. That's not even our business and if they put it in the wrong place we won't get it. Tell them not to put their key in the envelope in the blue box."

"Got it," Dana says, writing his words as fast as she can.

"If they don't write what's wrong with the car, that's okay because we'll just call them. But if they don't leave their name and number we can't do anything until they call us, and that could cost them another day in the shop. We don't want them to have to leave their car too long because that's not good for them or us.

Dana's head is swimming from all the (k)nots her boss was throwing at her. "Having been a student of Remember the Ice for a few months, Dana decides to try untying all of Joe's (k)nots. She rewrites the information he gave her in neat, positive bullet-points.

Exceptional Care for Your Valued Client

- Overnight drop-offs okay
- Park in the lot across the street ONLY
- MUST have envelope with:
    - Key
    - Contact information
    - Make and model of car, license plate
    - What's wrong with it
- Envelope goes in mail slot in our front door ONLY
- We will call them first thing in the morning – priority

Within an hour, Dana receives a frantic call from a woman whose car has broken down on the bridge halfway between work and home. A tow truck is on its way, but it will be well after 7 or 8:00 p.m. before they get the car back into town. She has no way of getting the car from her house to the garage in the morning and is desperate for a solution to what she sees as a gigantic *problem*.

Dana adopts a calm tone to go with her friendly voice and reassures the woman that the situation is straightforward and easy to address.

She begins with the center of the solution, and says directly and clearly, "Have your tow-truck driver bring the car directly to us."

"Won't you be closed? I can't get back in the morning; I have to be at work by 8:00 a.m."

"It's okay. We have a system for this, and we have made it as easy for you as possible," Dana continues to soothe the woman's anxiety. "I know it seems overwhelming right now. Know we are here to help you."

"Okay, thank you," the woman begins to calm down, too. "What do I need to do once I get the car over there?"

Section 1

Dana glanced at her notes. She had reinterpreted Joe's information about parking options and used the Remember the Ice method to make them clear and memorable.

"Tell the tow-truck driver to take the car to the parking lot across the street from us. It is the only place you can safely leave your car overnight," Dana said. "Remember, the lot across the street from our garage."

"Got it. Across the street."

"We will need your key and your permission to move your car into our shop tomorrow. So, write down your name and phone numbers, which car is yours, and what happened to it, and put the note with the key in an envelope. Did you get that? You must leave your key."

"Yes. You need my key."

"We have to talk to you before we can look at your car, so we must have your phone number."

"Okay."

"Now this bit is important," Dana says, to make sure she has the woman's attention, "Make sure you put the envelope through the mail slot in our front door. The door has our name on it in bright yellow. That mail slot is the only way to get the key to us."

Dana wonders about mentioning the blue box that belongs to the neighboring business, just to warn her customer in case of confusion. Then she laughs at herself; mentioning the box would create confusion. She knows better. What her customer needs is clear directions. And that's all she needs. When she walks up to the building she will be looking for bright yellow letters and a mail slot. Nothing else is part of the equation. Nothing else has been allowed into the instructions to clutter them.

"Thank you for your help. This is really overwhelming. I hope I can remember all that," the woman on the phone said.

Exceptional Care for Your Valued Client

"We are happy to help you. When you are here you will see the parking lot across the street, and you will remember the key and your name and number. It will all make sense to you. Just remember: Key and phone number in mail slot, bright yellow letters," Dana says, confident her customer will remember those details and all the rest once her car was safely deposited in the parking lot.

The following morning, Dana felt strangely satisfied to walk into the office and see the envelope on the floor under the mail slot. As predicted, the woman had remembered the key, her contact information, the make and model of her car, a description of what was wrong with it, and an expression of thanks to the woman on the phone who had been so calm and friendly and made the whole process run smoothly.

This interaction made Dana feel confident and happy about working with the next customer. As for the woman with the car, for years to come whenever anyone she knew needed a mechanic, she recommended Joe's shop.

Although Dana was the only person in the situation who had learned Remember the Ice communication skills, she was able to enhance and empower everyone else's experience through the practice of clarifying.

As with the instruction, "Don't put it in the blue box," other simple directions are prone to muddle the message. "Don't turn left at the bottom of the hill." Okay. Um, why bring "left" into it at all? If you tell me to turn right at the bottom of the hill, that's all I need to know to get me there. If you tell me to turn right and I take it upon myself to turn left, that's on me. Frankly, I deserve to get lost if I choose to ignore your directions.

The most effective and powerful way to communicate is to be clear, focused, and uncluttered. There is Power in the Clarity of your Articulation. The first step to achieving that clarity is to stop tying your messages up with (k)nots and figure out how to say the same thing in a more direct way that leaves no room for misunderstanding. This is especially important in customer service where understanding each other is the key to your entire relationship.

Section 1

"(K)not" and "don't" are just the beginning. (K)nots attach themselves to would-be powerful words and twist them into confusing and disempowering words that undermine our message and our efforts, and we let it happen without even thinking about it. Once you spend a little time identifying the (k)nots and don'ts around you, take a stab at the five "(k)notty" words in the next chapter that, together with "don't" make up what I call my "Hit List Six".

Exceptional Care for Your Valued Client

Section 1

Chapter 5

Strangling the Host

The toughest words to eliminate from your vocabulary will be (k)not and don't. We tend to cling to the belief that these words are necessary and effective. It's going to be a battle with your brain to drop them from your communication, be it written or non-verbal. You may be sitting here at the top of chapter five yet to be convinced. I'm hoping you take a good look at what (k)not does to good, empowering words and the stranglehold it places on them; then you will gain a better understanding of why I am so firmly against its use.

The next five *"(k)notty words"* are on my list for more than just the insidious way they invert your meaning. They add their own evil twist to the chaos. Each of the base words, "can," "could," "would," "will," and "should" imply an ability and willingness to cooperate. These base words are full of potential and possibility. Once you tie a (k)not onto them, the potential is shut down. Each word then carries a mixed signal to the brain, in this case: An implied ability and willingness to cooperate, but the refusal to do so.

This is extremely important to understand when it comes to exceptional care. When a representative of your organization uses one of these words, they are creating a negative experience for the customer.

- When *"can"* becomes *"can't,"* helpfulness becomes denial
- When *"could"* becomes *"couldn't,"* hope becomes failure
- When *"would"* becomes *"wouldn't,"* cooperation becomes rejection
- When *"will"* becomes *"won't,"* intention becomes refusal

"Should" is its own special brand of disempowering language. I will get to that later. For now, just know that it goes from bad to worse when you tie that (k)not to it. While "should" is an admonition loaded with

Exceptional Care for Your Valued Client

judgment, "*shouldn't*" is a reprimand – also loaded with judgment.

Note how the base word speaks of the future, yet once the (k)not is added to it, the resulting word has a different tense, either past or present. Note how (k)not shuts things down immediately. There is no future; it's all over now. I find this phenomenon fascinating.

Customers find it frustrating. When faced with a word like can't or won't from a customer service representative, they feel a sense of helplessness. No one likes to feel like their power has been taken away from them. Customers like to feel as though they have the power to shop where they choose and get the services they want and need. When people feel helpless they either become more aggressive and fight harder to get through the invisible barrier, or they walk away, completely unsatisfied, and spend their money elsewhere.

All five of these remaining *(k)notty words* are offensive and disempowering because they make an original "can do" message into its opposite. Remember, your brain hears the "can do" first and the reaction is positive. Then it dawns on your brain, the "not" is in there for a reason. Disappointment follows.

Do you allow your representatives to use any other offensive words or behavior? There is more than one way to illicit sour feelings about your business from a customer, and this collection of (k)nots falls right into that category.

Professional coaches know this. They make a point of driving home the destructive nature of the word "*can't*," and forbid its use. Coaches understand that if an athlete uses that word, they are going to accept failure before trying. "Can" is a word of motivation and inspiration. Tie a (k)not to it and you've just killed all that "can do" spirit.

A friend told me about an odd customer service situation her co-worker recently experienced. Peter had ordered a stamp from an office supply store that customizes them on-site. His company was in the practice of buying from this store weekly, and had ordered several stamps from

Section 1

them in the past without issue. As instructed, Peter showed up at the store to pick up the stamp the day after he ordered it.

The woman behind the counter looked at his paperwork and said, "You never called last night to confirm this was the stamp you wanted, so it's not done and I'm going on my lunch break soon."

Peter blinked. "I ordered the stamp right here, in person. May I ask why you needed me to go back to the office and call you to confirm it's what I wanted? I've never had to do that before."

"Look, I can't make a stamp unless I know it's what you want, and I told you to call by five o'clock to confirm it was right, and you didn't. So I didn't make the stamp."

Peter was sure he had received no such instruction, but wanted to avoid an argument. "Can you make the stamp now that I'm here to okay it? I can wait."

"I can't make it now. I'm going on my lunch. Come back later, like an hour."

"You want me to come back later for a stamp that takes five minutes to make?

"Well, no, you can come back any time before five and pick it up."

"But I'm here now."

"But you didn't call last night, so that's another day. I can't make a stamp without confirmation."

"I'm confirming it now. This is indeed the stamp I want made, and all the information is right. There's no one else in line. Can you make it while I wait, like you guys usually do?

"I don't make stamps while people wait and I can't make it before I go

Exceptional Care for Your Valued Client

to lunch." Peter and the woman went back and forth on the same point for several minutes, her stubbornness making him feel like he was being secretly filmed for a comedy show. Meanwhile, Peter did his best to avoid letting his sinking feeling of helplessness turn into anger.

Finally, he sought out a manager and recounted the story. "I just need to get back to the office with a stamp. Do you have anyone else who can make it for me?"

"No, I don't. She's the only one, and she has to go to lunch."

Peter's head was about to explode. "You see me in here every week. We spend at least $1,000 here every month. Are you telling me, you are unwilling to ask your employee to delay lunch by five minutes to make a stamp she was supposed to have ready by 5 p.m. yesterday?"

"I can't make her do it before she goes on break. It's the law. She can't go longer than five hours without lunch."

Peter stopped and looked at him with new eyes. A manager can at the very least encourage an employee to fulfill her job description, Peter thought to himself, but this man is refusing to help me. These people have no interest in keeping my business. Do they even care if I shop here? Have they ever cared about my loyalty?

Regardless of what they considered valid reasons, the woman who made the stamps and her manager made it very clear to Peter that when it came to meeting his needs, "I can't make it now," meant "I refuse to accommodate you" and "your business means nothing to us."

Needless to say, Peter's business has moved on. His annual $12,000 business with the office supply store may seem like peanuts to a large chain, but what the manager failed to consider is the fact that small business owners talk to each other. Small business owners appreciate the value of loyalty, efficiency, and doing a little extra for valued customers.

Section 1

In Peter's business, before anyone thinks of saying "can't," employees figure out how to work together to say, "We can make this happen," "This is what we can do for you," or "Can we do it this way for you?" Before a customer suspects a "won't," employees let their "can do" attitudes help them suggest win-win solutions so at the very least, the customer feels empowered.

If the woman responsible for making the stamp had stopped to hear herself speak and chosen to say "can" instead of "can't," her mind would have leapt ahead to start thinking of all the possibilities.

- "I can make that for you right away."
- "I can call you when it is ready."
- "I can push my lunch back to get this done; it will only take a few minutes."

The manager, who is empowered to do more for the customer, could have benefited from starting his response with "I can."

- "I can find another employee who knows how to make the stamp."
- "I can make the stamp."
- "I can deliver the stamp when it's done, or have it delivered."

He could have even said to himself, "I can keep our scheduling challenges to myself and avoid making the customer feel like he is inconveniencing us."

A stamp seems like a small commodity. How much is a loyal customer worth to you?

The following statements are infuriating to customers. They may be honest, but remember the brain registers the "can" first, and then the inverting (k)not turns it into the "I can, but I refuse."

Exceptional Care for Your Valued Client

- "I can't help you with that" – I have the power or ability to help you, but I refuse.

- "You can't leave that here" – You have the power or ability to leave that here, but I'm going to stop you.

- "We can't solve your problem" – We have the power or ability to solve your problem, but we are going to pretend otherwise.

- "We can't e-mail you the information" – We have the power or ability to e-mail you the information, but we just have no interest in expediting things for you.

- "We can't make an exception" – We have the power and ability to Make an exception, but we see no value in doing so to keep your business.

- "You can't talk to anyone else" – You have the power and ability to talk to other people here, but I'm going to prevent you from doing so.

Why do you think so many people bridle at the thought of being told what they "can't" do, where they "can't" go, how they "can't" be helped? I believe it's because "can't" is a dead-end statement that is tantamount to a wall with no way around it, no openings through which to find a solution, and no alternative paths to where the customer wants to go.

Historically, The great athletes and coaches have always known better than to use the word "can't." It is demoralizing, disempowering, and dissuades you from taking action.

In the same way that "can" is full of possibilities while "can't" is a dead end, "could" also promotes possibilities while *couldn't* deflate your customer's enthusiasm for dealing with you.

The fact of the matter may be that the doctor is slammed with patients who need to see him, and his receptionist has no way of knowing when he will be able to sit down to review test results for patients waiting at

Section 1

home, but there are two distinctly different ways to say that when an anxious patient calls.

"I'm sorry, I really couldn't say when he'll be able to look at your lab results and call you back." Said in a polite voice this may seem like a professional response. However, to the person on the other end of the phone, it sounds like "I could say when he'll be able to talk to you, but I choose to withhold that information."

How about: "I know you are anxious to hear the results, and as soon as the doctor is able to step away and review your results he will call you. Looking at his schedule, I see that he has no breaks between appointments for the next two hours. I will follow-up with him and one of us will give you a call."

When you offer up a phrase that includes a "can't" or a "couldn't" something else happens in your mind: You tend to hear yourself finalizing the situation and setting it in stone.

By now, I'm sure you get the picture. Attempt a few for yourself. Dissect these examples of "couldn't" and rephrase them. When would you be tempted to use them in your business? How many better ways can you come up with saying each of them?

Example:

"It couldn't be helped"

Equates to: "It could not be helped"

Is heard as: "It could be helped, but we failed. We are failures, but we're fine with that"

Replacement phrase: "It was out of our hands" or "It was beyond our control." Was it really?

Now you're accountable: "We considered several approaches. We looked into it, and from what we understand this is what happened."

Exceptional Care for Your Valued Client

Now you give it a go:

"We couldn't get it there on time."

Equates to:

Is heard as:

Replacement phrase:

Now you're accountable:

"We couldn't get it done."
Equates to:
Is heard as:
Replacement phrase:
Now you're accountable:

"He couldn't fix it."
Equates to:
Is heard as:
Replacement phrase:
Now you're accountable:

"I couldn't find it."
Equates to:
Is heard as:
Replacement phrase:
Now you're accountable:

I often get a chuckle when I hear *"wouldn't."* The classic, "I wouldn't do that if I were you…" has such predictable results, it's almost scary. What happens almost every time you say that? The person continues with whatever you're warning them to stop doing.

Section 1

"I wouldn't poke that bear with a stick if I were you." Poke, poke.

"I wouldn't tease your sister about that if I were you." Mom! She hit me!

Your store offers a service designed to make life easier for your customers. It's a nominal fee, and well worth it. Now that you know about (k)nots, would you persuade your customers to take advantage of this offer by saying:

"I wouldn't try doing it yourself if I were you. For $25 we'll take care of it for you."

Or

"We have a service that will take the hassle out of putting that together. We'll get it done quickly so that all you have to do is enjoy your new purchase."

Speaking of persuasion, "wouldn't" is frequently used to draw customers to a product or service, but it makes no sense when you break it down.

    Wouldn't you rather have us take care of that for you?

    Wouldn't you like faster service?

    Wouldn't you like more perks?

    Wouldn't you like to smell better?

Breaking it down, it goes like this:

    "Would not you like to smell better?" or: "Would you not like to smell better?"

Um, what? What do I say to that? "Yes, I would not like to smell better"

Exceptional Care for Your Valued Client

or "No, I would not like to smell better"? Either way, I stink.

If you want my attention, ask me "would you like to smell better?" Now I'm listening.

Be clear and direct with your customers:

> Would you rather have us take care of that for you?
>
> Would you like faster service?
>
> Would you like more perks?

Can you see the difference between the two ways of asking even the obvious questions? The use of "wouldn't" incorporates that built-in confusion and it invites consideration and delayed response, whereas the use of "would" demands an immediate answer.

Wouldn't I like a glass of wine with dinner? I'm unsure. Let me think about that for a minute.

Would I like a glass of wine with dinner? You have a cabernet that compliments what I just ordered? Yes, that sounds nice. I'll spend a little more on it since your question sparked an immediate and positive response.

To round out this list of offenders, let's talk about *"won't"* for a minute. The base word is "will," and it is one of the most positive and powerful words in our language. It means "this is going to happen." There is no room for doubt, there are no allowances for trying but failing, and no question that results are on their way.

Tie a (k)not to it and "will" becomes "won't," and all bets are off. Of course it means the opposite of "will," and that's the purpose of using a (k)not, right? Remember, though, your customer hears the "will" and then the (k)not. You let your customer's hopes rise, and then let them fall.

Section 1

"Won't" is a word of bull-headed stubbornness, and a refusal to entertain other possibilities.

   We won't carry that shoe after next week.

   The chef won't make substitutions.

The above statements may be true, but there's an art to communication that requires the ability to finesse information that may displease your customer.

Brad had just finished setting up a display of walking shoes from a new line that his father decided to carry when he looked up to see an older gentleman enter the store. Mr. Ross had been a loyal customer for as long as Brad could remember, and favored the brand that the new line was destined to replace.

Brad greeted him cheerfully, and after catching up with some small talk, asked what he could do for him.

"It's time to get another pair of these shoes," Mr. Ross answered, pointing to the pair he was wearing. "That will be my fourth pair just like them in seven or eight years or so."

"You have excellent timing, as usual, Mr. Ross," Brad said. "We have two pairs left in your size. I know you want to stick with this shoe, so you might want to consider buying an extra pair today while we still carry it. My dad and I have found a manufacturer that we believe makes a much better shoe. We are really excited to carry this brand, and it has the support you want. It will replace the other brand. I'll show you why I think you will like it as much, or more."

Whether Mr. Ross decided to try the new brand, buy the pair he came in for, or buy both remaining pairs in his size, Brad chose to avoid upsetting his customer. Why tell him what "won't" be available when what "is" and what "will" be available suits his needs?

Exceptional Care for Your Valued Client

Stacey was stuck in a challenging situation. As a server at one of the city's best restaurants, she took pride in the quality of the food. The chef insisted on fresh, local, sustainable ingredients, and had an amazing talent for blending flavors and textures that garnered the eatery rave reviews.

The only drawback was the chef refused to make substitutions to any of his dishes, and Stacey had trouble making "The chef won't do that" sound like a good arrangement. It was an extremely frustrating situation, and in Stacey's opinion the chef was being inappropriately stubborn and ran the risk of alienating customers.

Without the power to change his rules, Stacey had to put her opinions aside and figure out how to make the most of the situation for everyone involved. She was in the business to make money serving food to guests, so it was up to her to figure out how to make them excited about ordering it just the way the chef was bound and determined to make it.

After a few unsuccessful exchanges with guests who were unhappy being told they were unable to make changes to their meal, she sat down and decided to write down the reasons she trusted the chef's dishes "as is" so that she could focus on selling them that way.

At the beginning of her very next shift, Stacey found herself cheerfully anticipating the first guest to ask the chef to alter the dish for him.

"Of course I can ask him to do that for you," Stacey said, and then added in a provocatively suggestive tone, "but I have to tell you, I had a chance to sample the dish his way this afternoon, and I thought I'd died and gone to heaven. I was so pleased by the way the flavors blended, and it was like nothing I had had before."

That piqued her guest's interest, and after a minute of thoughtful persuasion, she had the guest drooling for the chef's creation. The more she practiced her positive sell, the less tension there was when a guest asked for a change and the happier each one left the restaurant.

Where there's a "will," there's a way. Where there's a "won't," there's no way.

Section 1

Now we come to one of my least favorite words in creation: Should.

"Should" is a bad, bad word. It is a bad, bad choice calculated to make the person it's spoken to feel bad, bad, bad about themselves. "Should" is used to predict a desired outcome, only it's more than that; it comes with implications like, "if things go my way, this should happen"; "if you do your job right, this should be the result"; "if you spend enough time working on it, it should pay off"; "if you know what you're doing, you should be able to fix the problem."

The predictive should comes with two results: When things happen the way they "should" have, whatever effort and skill was involved is inconsequential; it should have happened anyway, so what's the big deal? When things fall short of expectation the implied criticism is "what is wrong with you that you were unable to make what should have happened happen?"

Tie a (k)not onto it, and "shouldn't" is 10 times worse. The best it can be is "should not," which is a terrible, disempowering word loaded with judgment and reprimand. If you think about it, there is no reality that supports a "shouldn't." Only that which "should" happen can ever happen; because it does. And whatever "*is*" should be; because it "*is*". Anything that shouldn't have happened; had no way of happening. If it happened, it "should" have happened. To say an event shouldn't happen or shouldn't have happened is to claim that something will or has gone terribly wrong.

You may think that it's acceptable and even reassuring to tell a customer one of the following:

- It shouldn't be a problem

- It shouldn't take long

- It shouldn't cost too much

However, when you remember that your customer hears "It should be

Exceptional Care for Your Valued Client

a problem," "it should take long," and "it should cost too much" before the (k)not registers, you can see why this is a bad idea.

Avoiding poor word choice requires thinking about what you want to say before you throw out a statement that fills the space but falls short of what needs to be said. It requires an honest and direct approach, which is a lot more powerful than half-hearted commitments that commit you to nothing.

If you anticipate the job will run smoothly and present few challenges, say so. If you know from experience the job will be done quickly, say so. If you figure the job will be done within a specific budget, say so. If you suspect that there could be challenges, delays, or expenses outside the original estimate, say that, too. Your customer appreciates honesty as much as you do. Clear, honest statements demonstrate respect for your customer's time and intelligence.

It is tempting to fall back on throw-away common phrases, especially when you're busy or find yourself repeating the same information several times a day, and to throw a (k)not into a sentence instead of figuring out how to construct it properly the first time. However, if your goal is to make communication with your customers more efficient and to build a foundation of loyalty, respect and trust, then you have to learn to choose your words carefully and thoughtfully, every time you speak. This process begins by untying and eliminating all conceivable (k)nots from your vocabulary.

Now that I have introduced you to the practice of deconstructing your sentences in order to reconstruct them with power, clarity and integrity, I want to warn you that putting it all into practice is going to feel awkward. You're embarking on a process of learning and re-learning. I find it truly fascinating, and when you recognize it as you go through it, I think you'll be a little fascinated, too, and I hope you'll find yourself enjoying the ride.

Feel free to take some time today or tonight to play around with some of the exercises and challenges I presented here. Apply them to your

Section 1

unique business and the interactions you typically have with customers. I have included more of these games at the end of each section just to get your juices flowing and help get you thinking about how to reframe what you're wanting to say so you can continue to strengthen the ways in which this will assist you in *providing Exceptional Care for your valued client.*

Exceptional Care for Your Valued Client

Section 1

Chapter 6

No Means No

Have you heard the expression, "No means no"?

When you consider the fact that "There is Power in the Clarity of Your Articulation," I'd say it's pretty obvious the word "no" is one of the strongest tools in that clarity toolbox. It has the potential to be very empowering.

A simple "no" in response to a challenge from another, especially when you have already done your best to explain your reasoning with them can shut down an antagonist's attempt to wind you up, talk you into changing your mind, or coerce you into an unwise action.

In the face of whining, cajoling or disrespect, the power of a strong, clear "no" is the best way to close the discussion.

"Come on, dive off the cliff first. You know you want to."

"No."

However, if you use it in a customer service situation, "no" creates headaches. Saying "no" to a customer is disempowering to all parties, including yourself, and you're just asking for trouble. In this case, "no" means, "I have no interest in helping you."

Since "no" is one of my favorite words for direct speech, I'd like to introduce you to a friend and associate of mine, LuAnn Buechler, who is adamant about eliminating the word "no" from your *exceptional care* vocabulary.

LuAnn has more than 30 years experience in the hospitality industry, which encompasses just about every form and feature of customer service you can name. She has worked in almost every customer service

Exceptional Care for Your Valued Client

position imaginable, with the bulk of her experience forged in management positions overseeing convention services, catering, banquets, and sales.

Nowadays, LuAnn puts her Master's Degree in Hospitality Administration to work in her own business and also as an Adjunct Professor teaching Meeting and Convention Management at the University of Wisconsin, Stout. A Certified Meeting Professional (CMP), she has built a thriving business as an independent consultant.

If you know anything about meeting and convention management, then you have some idea of the logistics, details, and general jumping through hoops that need to be handled in order to deliver the product – a wildly successful event – to a smiling and satisfied client.

The ability to stay calm, gracious and cheerful as she manages multiple tasks and large groups of people while simultaneously putting out fires, attending to last-minute adaptations, and accommodating occasionally outrageous whims is a well-honed skill, refined over the years to an enviable standard of excellence that requires constant adherence to the underlying principles of client service.

LuAnn's company offers clients something she calls "Passionate Management of Customer Service." In practical terms this description translates into action as her team goes into the client's business to observe, audit and define existing customer service practices, assessing strengths and weaknesses in order to develop a comprehensive management plan that will support and direct the client's efforts to raise the bar, stand out from the competition, and make superfans out of all their customers.

With three decades in the hospitality industry under her belt, she has seen just shy of "it all," so when LuAnn says a word is unsuitable for exceptional care, I listen. She and I have strong customer service/exceptional care ethics in common, and we agree that empowering word choice is fundamental.

Section 1

Do you remember the point I made in the first chapter about signature moments, and how the key to great Exceptional Care is to create a Signature Moment with your client? According to LuAnn, "no" creates its own Signature Moment – and it is the last kind of moment you want your signature on.

LuAnn shuns the word "no" in customer service for the very reasons I encourage its use. It is the ultimate, unmistakable shut down. It is denial. It is refusal. It slams the door on the possibility of confusion. Clear and strong, "no" means "no."

The last thing a customer wants to hear is "no." Even if it is followed by an alternative suggestion, once that word is out of your mouth your customer is bridling with angst.

"When you say no to a customer," LuAnn says, "you immediately get their back up. Then their attitude becomes "oh yeah?" and you're in a no-win situation."

"No" is a word of denial. Worse, when you allow yourself to answer a question with a "no," the moment you utter the word you immediately lock yourself into the refusal mind-set. You have trapped yourself in a negative paradigm. Every attempt to cooperate after that is an afterthought, an emotional effort, and a pull on your energy.

You must enter every customer service interaction with a "can do" mindset, LuAnn says.

"You must remember at all times that it is easier to hold on to existing customers than it is to find new ones. And it is a whole lot easier than replacing the ones you have alienated."

She has a magnificent point. How do you attract new customers if the ones you have alienated are telling them you're unaccommodating?

So what's the best way to handle a customer who approaches you with a request or an inquiry?

Exceptional Care for Your Valued Client

LuAnn says, "Your immediate response needs to be: Yes. What is the question?"

I agree. Emphatically.

"Yes. What's the question?" See how that changes the mood and direction completely? I'll let you in on a little secret: This simple word response has just created a paradigm shift.

As LuAnn points out, when you react verbally with a "yes," you react mentally with a "yes." Your mind begins to work in constructive, *situation-solving* directions. Your whole demeanor becomes one of open helpfulness, and your thoughts work their way along solution paths in your brain. You also tend to have a better, happier attitude, which reflects on your face and is proof positive to your customer, that you are engaged, tuned-in, and actually care.

In every exceptional care scenario, LuAnn's words of wisdom begin at the beginning. "We may be unable to control our customer's attitude, however we can manage our own attitude and feelings. The mindset needs to be: What can I do? – Even if it's above and beyond the norm."

I love how our philosophies merge so beautifully! We come from different backgrounds and different experiences, and, we've both found what works – and it's the same thing.

"When you feel good about helping customers," LuAnn says, "you look for ways to help the person in front of you. You feel good about that success."

Regardless of your intention, if you begin with a "no," you waste time and energy back-tracking to the place where you can help the customer. By now, that customer is dealing with your disappointing "no" on top of whatever was concerning her in the first place. I guess you could "turn that frown upside down" for them with some genius move that makes everything better, but why bring frowns into it at all?

Section 1

Providing exceptional care for your valued clients means keeping those smiles on their faces, no frowns allowed.

Sometimes "Yes! What's the question?" means stepping outside your job description and maybe even your business to help.

"Yes, I can tell you how to get to the ferry landing. Our train will only take you about half way, but I'll write down which bus to get on at the final station, and that will get you right to the dock."

"Yes! What's the question?" gets part of its power from being open-ended. You have just invited your customer to ask for whatever they need, and you have just given yourself permission to respond in creative ways.

"Too often we react based on parameters that are arbitrary in some ways," LuAnn says. "Here are the lines, sure; however we can stretch them."

The key is to listen to what the customer is really asking for. We will definitely tackle paradigm shifts in the next few chapters, and here's a taste of how that simple first response can get you started on that.

Yvonne was ready to buy her first car. She had been kicking tires at a downtown car dealership for a couple of weeks, and the salespeople had helped her look at all the models in her price range, patiently running down available features and comparing specs as she made up her mind.

Finally, the day came when she was ready to buy. She had waited long enough and was now out of options.

The only challenge was she had no one to drive her down to the lot, and it was raining cats and dogs.

Being resourceful, and a little desperate, Yvonne decided to ask for help. "Do you think you could come get me? You know, like a test drive for the car? I would be able to drive myself home, of course."

Exceptional Care for Your Valued Client

Manny took a deep breath and fought like mad to keep the knee-jerk "Excuse me? Who do you think you are? The princess of somewhere I never heard of? What am I? Your go-for? I got nothing better to do? Get your own self down here" from shooting out of his mouth. Instead, he forced himself to hear what she was really asking for: Help getting to the lot so that she could buy a car from him.

That realization changed his paradigm.

What had initially felt like a self-indulgent and unreasonable request started to feel different; it started to feel like a young woman asking for a solution. Manny put her on hold and sat quietly while an idea ticked over in his head. He had to stay at the lot, but there might be another way. Within a moment he picked up the line again,

"Yvonne? I want to talk to my boss about working out a way to bring you down here. I will be as fast as possible. I know waiting on hold can be frustrating, so do you mind if I hang up and call you back in a few minutes?"

Manny walked across the showroom floor and knocked on the manager's office door. He explained the situation, and how their customer was stuck without a ride and would be for a while.

"Would it be okay to send the shuttle that we use for customers who have to leave their cars here for service? I know it's a bit unusual, but we drive out to that area quite often to take care of existing customers. If she buys a car from us, she will become one of those existing customers."

Manny's boss agreed, however, with a stipulation. "Remember, this shuttle has a specific service and customers who are getting their cars serviced come first. I'm only letting you do this because it's a special situation and no one else needs the shuttle right now." He checked his watch. "They will in an hour, though, so make sure you get this wrapped up by then."

Section 1

Manny called Yvonne and offered the solution. "Can you be ready in 20 minutes?"

Yvonne hesitated. "Is there any way it could come in an hour instead?"

Manny would have liked to have been able to say yes, but there was no way that would work. He also knew that a "no" could sour the situation, no matter how far outside the norm his offer appeared to be perceived.

He chose to say this instead: "I checked the schedule and have asked them to make an extra trip to pick you up. We're happy to do it, however this is the only window of time they have. If you need time to arrange for someone else to bring you down here, I can offer to hold the car on the lot until tomorrow."

This was all said with a cheerful voice, yet it also set the new boundaries. Yes, they were going above and beyond to help her; however, there were limits.

In the end Yvonne graciously accepted the ride at the shuttle's convenience, bought the car she wanted, and thought it only natural she would maintain her loyalty to the dealership service department for the life of her car – and the next one she bought from them.

Manny applied himself to finding a workable solution without ever having to say "no." It took some effort and a little creativity, but clients are worth it. They remember gestures large and small. The more you take the initiative to create solutions, the more natural it becomes. "No" may seem expedient, but consider how much more effective a simple statement can be, especially when it shows you have been paying attention.

"No" may seem expedient, yet consider how much more effective a simple statement can be, especially when it shows you have been paying attention.

LuAnn and I would like to make a very important distinction here. Merely replacing the word "no" with a nicer way to shut the customer up is

Exceptional Care for Your Valued Client

nowhere near good enough. You are still confronting them with an impervious wall. The key to creating the right "no" message is to make sure the result moves the customer in the right direction. The goal is to present a possible answer to their situation, and thus maintain a positive connection with your customer.

According to LuAnn, and I agree wholeheartedly, one of the most frustrating experiences for any customer is running into the wrong person in your company. The "wrong" person is a roadblock. He has a very clear understanding of the scope of his job, but only task-by-task. He has no idea how tasks outside his job description are handled, and lacks the curiosity or initiative to find out who does know.

When asked by a customer for help or information that falls outside his job description, his response is a "no" and a blank expression or a less than useful explanation, albeit apologetic – if you're lucky.

"Do you know where the ladders are?"
"I'm sorry. I work in the paint department."

"Can you help me choose some ground cover for my front yard? I know very little about the differences between them.
"I just water the plants."

"Do you know if I can get a different fabric on this?
"Um, I'm new here."

"Do you know if you will be open on Labor Day?"
"I just do deliveries."

"Can you answer some questions about my invoice?"
"Oh, you called the front office. Sorry."

In other words: Can you help me? No – That's Not My Job.

And what does the customer hear? No – That's My Job (but I refuse to do it).

Section 1

If you recognize any of this in your own business, then it's way past time to pay attention; it's time to take action.

Those answers are conversation-enders. Do you know what else they are? Deal-breakers. You just broke the deal you made with your customer that you would provide what he needs when he needs it. With that deal broken, your customer feels free – and happy – to go somewhere else.

People in customer service roles need to learn how powerful these simple phrases are:

"I will find out for you."

"I will find an associate who can help you."

"I will connect you with the right person."

"I will find a better resource for you."

In other words: Can you help me? Yes – By finding out how first. The "how" may be asking another person, fetching another person or leading the customer to another person, and that's fine. That's wonderful; that's part of the process that leads to the help they can point to.

If your customer stumbles into the wrong department, you want them to circulate quickly and painlessly until they get to the right person or the right department for their needs, right? It's important to arm each person in your business with the ability to identify the customer's need and maneuver her to the right resource.

Department stores make sure there are signs displayed prominently throughout so that customers can find their way around. They want the teenagers to be able to find the hot new jeans, even if they stumble into housewares. Salespeople need to know where those jeans are, too, as do the cashiers, the security guards, the managers, the people spritzing

Exceptional Care for Your Valued Client

passersby with perfume – you name it, if they're on the floor, they need to be able to tell every teenager walking through where to find the jeans. And, as we've been saying, if the security guard has no idea where the jeans are, he needs to be able to direct the teenager to the cashier or salesperson who does.

To be able to function like this requires the right people in the right roles, a strong sense of teamwork, a shared interest in the products or services being sold, and enough pride and loyalty in your employees that they want to see the business succeed. These are the factors that create what I call the "perfect customer service storm," and by the end of this book you will have an understanding of how to use the Remember the Ice tools to whip up that storm in your own business.

Do everything you can to help your customers navigate through your business. Begin with informed employees who, at the very least, are resourceful enough to find another person to help.

The old saying, "The Customer is Always Right" is actually wrong. "Always" is an absolute, which has no place in human experience, especially customer interactions. Customers are frequently wrong. They have unreasonable expectations, or lack enough information to make a judgment call, or simply have no idea what the scope of your services is.

Anyone can walk into a vegetarian market and demand to see the selection of lamb; being a customer makes him no more right than it makes him a Martian. It's how you handle that customer that makes or breaks you.

"Do you have lamb kabobs?"

"We're a vegetarian market, so we carry meatless products. We have some really hearty vegetable kabobs over here. Can I show you our selection?"

"I want lamb kabobs. I'm the customer, I hate vegetables, and I want lamb kabobs."

Section 1

"There's a butcher nearby with a good reputation. Would you like me to write down the name of his shop and where it is?"

There are indeed many ways to convey "no" without saying "no." Obviously, there are the ones that are designed to shut the customer up, thereby shutting him down. Now we're going to look at the ways you can confirm the "no" but keep the topic open for further exploration.

Actually saying the word "yes" is just one way to avoid saying "no." The key is to offer a helpful response that leads to a helpful action. Whether you're using redirection to avoid saying "no" or you're actually saying "yes," you must keep the situation moving in the right direction: meeting the customer's needs.

Pop quiz: It's your first day working in the electronics department at a large store. You know just enough about computers to get by, but you're still learning about the specs for each of the different models on the floor. A customer walks up to you with very specific questions about memory, processors and RAM. Do you say:

A: "I don't know" and wait for him to walk away

B: "I don't know," shrug, and walk away

C: "Wow, I wish I knew, but I'm new. Sorry."

D: I'm going to get someone right away who will be able to answer your questions. What is your name, sir? Brian? Would you mind waiting right here for just a minute, Brian, while I get another associate? I'll be right back."

Let's go back to the notion that "no" creates its own Signature Moment. Ideally, a Signature Moment is an experience you create for your customer that leaves an emotional impression on them. If they were impressed by your knowledge of wine pairings, they will remember that little pleasure when they think of your restaurant, and they'll feel attached to you personally through a sense of confidence in your

Exceptional Care for Your Valued Client

opinions about wine. That human touch benefits the business and the server.

"Where would you like to go to dinner tonight, honey?"

"Let's go back to that place where they had the server that recommended that pinot noir. Remember that? How it was the perfect choice?"

"Yeah, yeah, I remember! That was so good. There was a chicken dish I wanted to order.

Let's see if we can get a table and ask for him again. What was his name?"

"Mark. Remember?"

"Yeah, Mark. Man that was a great meal. That was the best wine. I wonder what he'll suggest for that chicken. It sounded kind-of spicy."

"Let's see if Don and Barb want to go. They love experiencing new restaurants, especially when they know what they're talking about."

Good customers return. Good customers bring other good customers with them next time. As you can see, it was the Signature Moment that created the good customer and got the ball rolling.

The server, Mark, created the ideal Signature Moment. He was helpful, insightful, and created a connection with his customers.

Flipping this concept for a moment, what do you think happens when you say "no"? What kind of Signature Moment evolves from that response, even if it comes with a smile and an "I'm so sorry I have to say that" shrug or commiserating sad-eyed look and "I wish we could" sigh.

After 30 years of face-to-face time with all kinds of customers, LuAnn can tell you with full confidence exactly what happens when you tell a

Section 1

customer "no." Whether they become combative or remain calm, push for a resolution or simply walk away, their opinion of you and your business takes a nose-dive.

In our culture, the accepted notion is: customer service is such a basic, rudimentary skill; if you are unable to rise to that minimum challenge then there is something seriously wrong with you and your business.

People remember their Signature Moment with you; that's the point. The couple who reminded each other of the wine-pairing server they thought was so competent will also remind each other of the salesperson in the pet store they thought was so incompetent.

"Hey, so, do you still want to add a couple of fish to that tropical tank we have downstairs? It would be pretty cool to have something new for when your nephews get here. They love that fish tank."

"Totally. I was reading about one kind that would do really well with what we already have, and they're supposed to be this incredibly amazing blue. I'd want to see one first, and I want to make sure we have the right equipment. Do you think they'll be able to help us where we bought the last fish and the new filter?"

"That place? Do you remember what a hassle that was? I felt like we were asking for the moon. We just wanted to get that one brand of food, and someone to show us how to hook up the filter."

"Yeah, I remember that chick. She had no desire to help us, whatsoever. Everything was a no, it was all too hard."

"Was she brain-dead, or just rude?"

"Who knows? Who cares? Let's check out that other place on the other side of town. They're smaller but I hear they'll special-order a fish for you if they need to."

"Let's go now."

Exceptional Care for Your Valued Client

The young woman in the fish store who let this couple down only said "no" twice in the hour they were there bombarding her with questions; once to whether they carried a specific brand of fish food, and once to whether she could show them how to hook up the filter. She missed the opportunity to develop loyalty and trust in her customers, and to come across as knowledgeable and capable. Instead, she signed away the moment.

"No" may be seem like the immediate answer and the most efficient way to end a line of inquiry, but it creates the most work when it's time to recover from its use, repair its damages and redirect the path you and the customer started walking down.

Take note of when you indulge in the knee-jerk reaction to say "no," especially when you mean "no." There are times in every business where "no" sums up the truth. There's still no excuse for using it.

"Are you open on Sundays?"

No.

"Do children get to go in for free?"

No.

"Do you have a valet service?"

No.

"This coupon expired last week. Will you still honor it?"

No.

Can you see what each of these exchanges has in common? There's nowhere to go after each "no." Are you going to make your customer drag the information they're looking for out of you, like getting blood from a stone?

Section 1

No!

"Are you open on Sundays?"

"We're closed on Sundays, but we're open from 10am to 7pm on Saturdays and 9am to 6pm Monday through Friday. Is there anything I can help you with in the meantime?"

"Do children get to go in for free?"

"Admission for children and seniors is half-price. Actually, the matinee is the best family value. Would you like to see our schedule?"

"Do you have valet service?"

"There are two parking lots on this street with valet service. One is two doors down to the left of us, and the other is a block past it. Both have security and are well-attended."

"This coupon expired last week. Will you still honor it?"

"We are unable to accept expired coupons; however, we do offer new coupons periodically, and if you need the service in the meantime, our prices are very competitive."

If you're interested in staying in business, then it's time to understand that you have an obligation to connect with your customers, draw them in, serve them, and make sure they know in their gut that they want to deal with you, come back to you, and send people to you.

Lay the foundation for these relationships by paying attention to your word choice. Eliminate the (k)nots from your vocabulary. Toss "no" overboard. Get rid of the phrases and responses that shut your customer down. Instead, choose words and phrases that come from the "yes" mind-set and build a loyal following.

Knowing which words to get rid of is just the beginning. In order to fully

Exceptional Care for Your Valued Client

reap the benefits, you have to know how to replace them. First, you have to know why. After you know why, you will be able to take it all in on a gut level, practicing until the choice to use empowering language becomes automatic.

I'm really excited about the next chapter; we're going to get down to the nitty-gritty of empowering and disempowering word choice. This information is going to keep you motivated to make the effort to change the way you speak and the way you teach your employees to speak to your customers.

Section 1

Section 1 Exercises

Raising the bar on "(K)notty Word" Awareness

You have been introduced to the concept of identifying and re-framing the "(K)notty Words". Now it is time to roll up your sleeves and dive in to the arena of your company documents, marketing materials, website content, memos, signs around the office, etc… and identify the (k)notty language that is currently there.

Take a look around your office, computer, day timer, or post it notes; and see what the "(K)notty Word" landscape looks like.

(Remember, this is just the written word at the moment.)

Take the first five you come across and re-frame them. Re-write the message. Remember to focus on the intended message. Is there confusion when the "(K)notty Words" are left in there? See what kind of adjustment you notice when you remove them.

Exceptional Care for Your Valued Client

Next, listen intently for the cacophony of (K)notty Words that reverberate around in the office, break room, shop area, construction site, restaurant or sales floor.

Have you heard any of the examples from Chapter 1 being bandied about?

"He's not here."

"This guy's not happy."

"It's not ready."

"It's not going to be cheap."

"It's not a problem."

"It's not an easy thing to fix."

"She's not interested."

"That's not something we do."

"That's not my department."

"We're not able to see you today."

Take a look at each of these, and re-frame them. Write out your empowering alternative on the lines below. (And consider using your new statements and responses right away.)

He's not here: ....
....

This guy's not happy: ....
....

It's not ready: ....
....

Section 1

It's not going to be cheap: ....

It's not a problem: ....

It's not an easy thing to fix: ....

She's not interested: ....

That's not something we do: ....

That's not my department: ....

We're not able to see you today: ....

Remember; repetition is the mother of skill. Stay engaged in the process of re-framing your message by using empowering words to articulate more effectively. The most important thing you can do is to keep raising your awareness of "(K)notty Words" and replace them.

Exceptional Care for Your Valued Client

Section 2

SECTION 2

Learning How to Speak and Act to Empower Yourself AND Your Client

Chapter 7: Learning How You Learn in Order to Re-Learn

Chapter 8: What's Wrong With Always Right?

Chapter 9: Shoulds, Absolutes, and More Words to Watch Out For

Chapter 10: Respectful Elegance via your Employees

Chapter 11: Respectful Elegance and the Power of Self-Esteem

Chapter 12: Best Practices. Exceptional Care Words and Behavior

Exercises for Section 2

Exceptional Care for Your Valued Client

Section 2

Chapter 7

Learning How You Learn in Order to Re-Learn

In the first section of this book I wanted to give you some word choices to sink your teeth into, so you could start practicing them and reap the rewards right away. How did it feel to check your words as you formed each sentence? When you untied a (k)not and replaced it with a better word, how did it taste in your mouth?

If you're like most people, it was a little awkward at first. You may have found yourself feeling frustrated, rolling your eyes, or playing the part of the skeptic. You may even believe, while they're appropriate for customer service exchanges, these concepts hold no real place of value in your personal communication style. If you recognize these concepts as the keys to providing Exceptional Care for your valued client, can you recognize their potential when applied to the rest of your life?

When you practice good word choice and strong communication skills in one area of your life, it branches out into the rest of your life.

This is an important point to understand. In fact, I would like you to embrace it. You will get the most out of using these tools to improve customer service skills if and when you consciously apply them across the board, in every aspect of your business, in other professional interactions, in your personal relationships, in your recreational activities, and especially when you are someone else's customer.

The more skeptical you are, the more I like it. Resistance is good. It means you're going to really dig in and use your brain, challenge what I tell you, test every step, and get the full experience out of learning to use each new concept. This, in turn, will make you a better teacher as you strike out and train the people you trust to attend to the needs of your customers.

You have had your lifetime to date to develop the communication skills you use today. Changing and enhancing them will require a learning

Exceptional Care for Your Valued Client

process. At first, it will feel awkward and forced. That is okay. At this stage it is awkward and forced. You are stepping out of the automatic ways of speaking that are second nature and require a minimum of thought into deliberate diction that demands focus and careful word selection. Because making decisions about your words as you speak according to someone else's dictates is in effect retraining your brain, the learning process is essentially the same as taking on any other skill.

Consider your present level of communication your foundation, or your starting point. It has brought you this far. What I teach is refinement and growth – refinement and growth that will take you to a powerful new level of communication with unlimited potential for success. The goal is to make your word choice and communication skills serve and empower you.

Let's take what you have now, build on it, cut out the bits that fall short of successful, and move everything forward because, as I tell almost every person I meet, "There is Power in the Clarity of Your Articulation." You may think your articulation is clear enough as it is. I'm here to help you polish it up to a shine and show you the difference.

Recently, a friend of mine friend shared an analogy from a co-worker. Imagine you are driving through the desert and there are bugs on your windshield, and sand and dirt have mixed with the bugs, sticking and smudging on the glass. You can see where you're going, and you can enjoy the vistas around you. You're used to the quality of the glass you're looking through. But then you stop at a gas station and clean the windshield. When you get back in the car and start to drive, the difference in how clearly you can suddenly see the world around you is astounding. You were fine before, however that was because you had yet to realize the difference.

Why limit yourself to adequate conditions when clean, clear conditions enhance your experience on so many different levels – and are so easy to create?

This chapter is about learning how you learn, so you can ultimately become an effective teacher and strengthen the communication skills

Section 2

of as many people around you as possible. Whether you are a company of one, oversee a dozen customer service representatives, or set the policies and standards for hundreds of employees who are the first point of contact with your customers, you have the power, through your representatives, to influence the way each and every person feels about doing business with you.

In the first chapter we talked about the importance of customer loyalty, especially in challenging economic times. Communication builds connections, and connections build relationships. Loyalty grows out of relationship. It all revolves around perception. As a customer, am I being treated with respect? Which words and behaviors reassure me that I am? Which words and behaviors trigger suspicion or disappointment? Can I trust this person in front of me, let alone the company behind him?

Communication is a complex art-form, with many facets that intertwine and mix together to express what you say and what you mean. Whatever you're doing now, there's room for improvement. And I could almost guarantee you're going to have to pay special attention to adopting what I teach, and it will take time and attention. Know it is worth it.

There's a very good reason for that awkward feeling I mentioned earlier. There's even a scientific explanation for it. That feeling is part of the Process of Education and Re-Education as researched and theorized by Dr. Maxie C. Maultsby, Jr., who introduced it to me roughly 35 years ago. A brief detour into learning how you learn will, I hope, help you commit to using the tools offered in this book – and having fun while you do it.

When it comes time to teach other people in your business how to use these tools to improve their customer service skills, you will have the advantage of insights shared here. The really great teachers pay attention to how their students learn. Since you are teaching yourself how to use the concepts in this book, I'm going to teach you how you learn.

We go through an Education Process every time we learn a new skill and a Re-Education Process when we change it up. There's no escaping it. The process can be disarming and uncomfortable, but that can make it exciting

Exceptional Care for Your Valued Client

and interesting, too. If you have an understanding of what's happening to you in the middle of the process of education and re-education, you can identify where you are on the path to mastering a skill. I find that fascinating.

Actually, I find *everything* to do with the psychology of word choice fascinating. It's a passion that has navigated me through four decades of learning, teaching, practicing and counseling.

It has taken me on a journey of careers in the mental health and motivational-speaking industries, in sales, marketing and networking, and as a small business owner. Today I address groups of anywhere between three and 3,000 people, work with small businesses and large corporations, and provide one-on-one coaching for individuals. Through it all, my understanding and unique take on the Psychophysiology of Words has strengthened and enhanced my work, my clients, and my relationships. Using the tools and concepts I teach has been the backbone of my success.

My official education began in college and continued through graduate school as I was introduced to ground-breaking research and cutting-edge theories like Rational Emotive-Therapy, Rational Behavior Therapy, Cognitive-Emotive Dissonance, Neuro-Linguistic Programming and Neuro-Associative Conditioning systems, by many of the same psychologists who developed them.

Dr. Maxie C. Maultsby, Jr., was the director of the Outpatient Psychiatric Clinic at the University of Kentucky's medical school when I was there in 1975 for the Certification Program in Rational Behavior Therapy. He was my mentor, and taught me to understand and embrace the concept of Cognitive-Emotive Dissonance, which describes that weird, anxious, funky feeling you get when you try doing something you normally do automatically in a whole new way.

Let me explain by zooming out to a bigger picture, and begin by outlining the Process of Education. Keep in mind I am over-simplifying some pretty complex research and theory development for the sake of expediency. The Process of Education goes as follows:

Section 2

1. Intellectual insight
2. Practice
3. Emotional Insight
4. Personality trait information

Intellectual insight is achieved when you understand the theory that supports what you want to learn. Practice is just as it sounds; this is the stage where you put that theory into practice. It is the hands-on stage that translates the intellectual into the physical, binding them together to get you to the next stage.

Emotional insight develops once you have spent enough time practicing the new skill to feel comfortable with it. When it becomes second nature, you have reached personality trait formation. At this point you perform the task automatically, often subconsciously, as if you had been doing it your whole life.

Learning to speak follows this process, if you assume that a very young child observes how the people around him communicate and then makes a decision to learn how to do it, too. I love watching small children on the cusp of breaking into language. They watch speaking faces intently, focusing on their mother's mouth shape as she makes a word or their father's expression as he repeats a sound. They listen carefully to tone and absorb every nuance. Often, they reach out to touch the face that is talking to them, as if to feel how to make the words come out. I could be convinced they are developing intellectual insight in order to really start practicing.

When a child starts practicing speech, I dare you to attempt to stop her! As soon as she discovers the power of words, she becomes greedy for new sounds, more ways to express herself and more ways to get the reactions and responses words bring. Children learn quickly: words hold a lot of power.

Pretty soon, she's talking non-stop, almost without thinking. Prattling on and on about the day and the car and the ride in the car and the

Exceptional Care for Your Valued Client

clouds in the sky and the rain from the sky and the water in the pool and the flowers and the bunnies and everything else she can think of in a steady stream of consciousness; she demonstrates emotional insight and personality trait formation.

In time, the child develops self-control, and thinks before speaking, or at least becomes more selective about what comes out of her mouth. If only more of us had the wisdom to refine that quality.

A child learns how to speak and communicate by observing and interacting with the people around her. If she is exposed to people whose language is helpful, she will speak the language of helpfulness. If she is exposed to people whose language is confrontational, she will speak the language of confrontation. She and her language will rise to the level of the people and language around her. Retraining a person to speak professionally, casually, meekly, assertively or whichever adverb represents customer service in your business, begins with correcting individual word choice.

The Process of Re-Education builds onto the Process of Education with a major shift and an additional step:

1 New Intellectual Insight
2 Converting Practice
3 *Cognitive-Emotive Dissonance*
4 New Emotional Insight
5 New Personality Trait Formation

Basically, these are the steps you have to go through to adapt your existing skills to a new setting or a new set of requirements. You are building on your skills, but at the same time changing them at a fundamental level so that they will serve you better and more completely where you are today, and where you want to be tomorrow.

Converting Practice is identifying how and why a skill needs to change, and then practicing the new application.

Section 2

Take a dancer who suddenly has to perform the mirror image of the routine she practiced a million times. She will feel awkward stepping to the left when she used to practice stepping to the right, but if she is vigilant and focused it will take fewer repetitions to convert the practice of moving left to moving right than it did to learn the original routine in the first place. Once the original routine has been learned, switching it up will feel strange but the learning curve will be a lot less steep. The act of practicing it the new way is the converting practice. When she performs the routine the new way, the hyper-aware state she will be in is Cognitive-Emotive Dissonance in action.

When you train a customer service representative to be more professional, for example, you might begin by targeting and eliminating the key words that are the opposite of professional, like street slang and casual expressions. Adopting the professional phrase you want her to use will feel awkward to her and sound awkward to you at first, yet after enough Converting Practice and going through Cognitive-Emotive Dissonance, it will become second nature and flow smoothly. Here are some examples, going from a street slang level, to casual expressions, to professional statements:

1. Yo, what's up?
Hey there, Mrs. Jones!
Good morning, ma'am (or Ms. Jones)

2. Later, man
See you next time
I look forward to seeing you again soon

3. Don't get crazy; back off
It's not my fault; calm down
I understand your frustration, and am working diligently on a solution

4. ...if that's cool
If that's okay with you
Is that an acceptable arrangement?

Exceptional Care for Your Valued Client

5. I dunno
I don't know but I'll check
Would you excuse me for a moment while I find out for you?

6. You like your food?
Was everything okay?
How did you enjoy your meal this evening, Mr. and Mrs. Reynolds?

To step away from words and communication for a minute, I'd like to share a personal story I frequently use in my keynote talks and trainings because I find it to be a near perfect example of the Processes of Education and Re-Education.

"When I was a teenager I was thrilled, excited, nervous, and a whole set of similar emotions every time I thought about finally learning to drive a car. I made plans in my head like any kid my age, imagining all the places I'd drive to, who I'd take with me, and where I'd take my dates on Friday nights. Learning to drive meant one thing: Independence.

"I knew that being able to drive was destined to change my life, and it was something I desired more than just about anything else in the history of my existence. However the desire to drive is a long way from actually driving, and, like everyone else, I had to go through the Process of Education before I could greet that life-changing destiny.

"So I signed up for and attended the drivers' education classes in my community. Dutifully, I paid attention in class, took notes, read pamphlets and rule books, studying the theory of driving so that when I got behind the wheel of a car I would know what to do. I will never forget the movies they showed us – loaded with blood and gore – that were designed to scare us into obeying the traffic rules, just in case we needed extra incentive.

"At the end of the class, I took the written test to prove I had gained the Intellectual Insight necessary to drive a car.

Section 2

"And then the glorious day came for me to put the theories into practice. I slid behind the wheel of my father's car, heart pounding and hand shaking just a bit. I took about 10 full minutes checking gears, gauges, mirrors, seat belts, gears, gauges, mirrors, seat belts, over and over.

"When I finally felt ready, I let out the clutch and started down the drive. As I maneuvered through the streets around my home, I was hyper-aware of everything going on around me. All of my senses were heightened, and my conscious thoughts were focused on what was going on inside the car, outside the car, right in front of the car, behind the car, across the field to the left of the car… I took "paying attention" to a whole new level.

"With each succeeding drive after that first one, I became more and more comfortable and relaxed considerably. The more I practiced driving, the more confident I became. My Emotional Insight was getting stronger.

"I think we can all admit that after enough years of driving, some of it becomes automatic, left to our subconscious mind to carry us through the motions. Instead of consciously reminding ourselves to check the rearview mirror every five to eight seconds, we glance over there automatically.

"The act of driving and its components have become personality traits. All that practice formed habits that are now traits.

"If you have had the same commute for long enough, you probably spend lengths of your drive almost on autopilot. Have you ever parked your car at work, only to wonder how you got there?

"Fast forward a few years to a point where I have been driving for a while. I am a young man, finishing my senior year in college, and I have decided to travel before diving into graduate school.

"I found myself in London, staying at a hostel with other youths. A couple of young women, also from America, expressed a desire to rent a car and drive out to the country for the day, however they were wary of driving on the other side of the road. Having the confidence young

Exceptional Care for Your Valued Client

men have in their ability to master anything in the universe (except perhaps women), I volunteered to be their driver.

"When I slid behind the wheel for the first time in a foreign country, it was like being in my father's driveway for the first time all over again. My *New Intellectual Insight* on this day came down to the fact I knew that everything was on the opposite side; all the mechanisms in the car were on the opposite side, all the street signs were on the opposite side, and all the traffic I had to pay attention to was on the other side. And there was a pretty girl next to me, also on the opposite side. I identified what I wanted to learn as new behavior, what I had to pay attention to in order to adapt to driving on the other side of the road. I knew the theory of everything I would have to do to swap over and drive safely.

"In this example, my *Converting Practice* was realizing I had to change my behavior to accomplish my goal. I knew if I continued to behave as though I was in the U.S., I would have major challenges; therefore, I had to practice something different, namely looking for the middle line over my right shoulder instead of my left.

"Once again, I was hyper-aware of my surroundings as I pulled away from the curb. In the process of reminding myself over and over to check for that line over my right shoulder, make sharp left turns and wide right turns, and all the other things to remember I was experiencing some degree of *Cognitive-Emotive Dissonance*."

"Cognitive-Emotive Dissonance is the fun part. On that day in London, I achieved several goals. I developed the ability and confidence to drive anywhere in the world, regardless of which side of the road I find myself on. I found my way to a beautiful area of the English countryside that I would have missed had I lacked the courage to try something new. And possibly best of all, I had a wonderful day with two pretty girls who thought I was their hero."

The thing is, once you begin to tackle new skills and recognize the high you get from mastering them, you start to crave more experiences that will stretch your knowledge and place you squarely in that off-kilter

Section 2

zone. As if addicted to the thrill, you will seek opportunities to push yourself. When you know how you learn, it becomes more exciting to be in the process of learning than you could imagine before doing it.

There are many areas in exceptonal care that involve the Process of Education and Re-Education, from the most basic tasks to the most complicated. I'll show you what I mean.

Answering the phone

Every person in your business who answers the phone was taught by someone somewhere how to deliver a professional greeting. They each had a first time on that phone, a first call where they recited the words into the phone exactly the way they were told. It was done deliberately, carefully, and self-consciously. There was complete focus on getting it right. Within a short time – 10 calls for some people, maybe 25 for others; more or less depending on the individual – the correct way to answer the phone became automatic. The Process of Education was in play:

1. Intellectual Insight – listening to instructions about what to say on the phone.
2. Practice – answering the phone and speaking the words.
3. Emotional Insight – beginning to feel comfortable with the words as they flow.
4. Personality Trait Formation – saying the words automatically without thinking about them.

Now, what if the person who learned to answer the phone for Company A moves on to a job at Company B where he has to answer the phone for them instead? He has to learn what his boss wants him to say, and then focus on doing it right without slipping up.

"Good morning; Company A; this is Roger; can I help you?" is no longer the right way to answer the phone. Roger's brain is on hyper-drive: Lift up the receiver the same way, say this instead of that, use the same tone of voice.

Exceptional Care for Your Valued Client

1. New Intellectual Insight – knowing he is answering the phone with a different script.
2. Converting Practice – remembering and practicing "It's a beautiful day at Company B; my name is Roger; how can I help you today?"
3. Cognitive-Emotive Dissonance – consciously checking to make sure the right words are being used, and feeling really weird about it.
4. New Emotional Insight – feeling comfortable and natural saying the new greeting.
5. Personality Trait Formation – saying the words automatically without thinking about them.

The same process can be applied to using cash registers and credit card machines, processing orders, troubleshooting, and every other customer service task you can think of. In fact, I challenge you to think of 10 to 20 tasks within your business that invite the opportunity for Education or Re-Education. While you're at it, can you identify any individuals who could benefit from a patient walk-through or retraining on any of these tasks?

Are you impatient to move on? We'll get back to the tools you can start practicing right away in the next chapters.

The challenge will come with taking the information in on a level that enables you to use it, practice it, and apply it to everyday interactions. Changing habits, especially communication habits, requires awareness, work, and vigilance. The pay-offs can be huge. You will get out what you put into it; the more effort you make to demonstrate respect and appreciation for your customers, the more they will be drawn to doing and repeating business with you.

In order to change the way you communicate, even at ground level, you have to begin by being hyper-aware of the words you choose, and vigilant about applying them. It requires effort, and can be rewarding and exhausting at the same time. Any time you tune into what you're doing with the goal of identifying what needs to change so you can improve, there's going to be a certain level of honesty and humility required. There's also a learning curve.

Section 2

Keep this in mind when it's time to train anyone who is in place to represent your business to your customers. We're going to focus again on word choice as the key to providing exceptional care for your valued client as we move into a discussion about the difference between empowering and disempowering words, how to identify them and how to choose to use or eliminate them.

Exceptional Care for Your Valued Client

Section 2

Chapter 8

What's Wrong With Always Right?

"The customer is always right."

This statement is so prevalent in our society, we tend to accept it without question, without batting an eyelid. And yet, it fails to stand up to scrutiny.

Is it a true statement? No. It is a fallacy. You may have heard it a million times, and you may have said it a million times. But think about it. "The customer is always right." Really? Always? All ways and always? In every way? There's no chance a patient could be wrong about the cause of his symptoms, or a do-it-yourselfer, having failed to take your advice to buy the right tools, could be the one in the wrong?

It is yet another example of common usage clouding our judgment; we use it without thinking, and it's to our detriment.

Does repetition make an incorrect statement true? No. So let go of this one. This is what I call a disempowering statement, and I'll show you why it's okay to drop it from your business philosophy. Then you'll be able to focus on rephrasing what it means to you in a more empowering way. Taking the disempowering and retooling it to be empowering is a skill-set that can make huge differences in your business, starting immediately with providing exceptional care.

Saying, thinking or believing the "customer is always right" implies she knows more about your business than you do; that somehow she has more information about how to price your goods and supplies appropriately, how much time different tasks require, and what the individual skill-sets of each of your employees are. Really? Could this be right? No. It is ridiculous to consider that prospect. And yet we repeat this statement like a mantra, placing it on an altar and bowing down to it like it is some kind of guiding light, when in reality it is impractical and

Exceptional Care for Your Valued Client

encourages disrespectful behavior from your customer. This phrase is disempowering for you and your employees. It puts you on the defensive when you are unable to acquiesce to your customer's demands.

You need a better way to say what you mean.

How does it feel when a customer comes into your place of business and starts telling you how things "should" happen, "should" be priced, "should" be designed for her benefit? Do you welcome this as an empowering encounter, or do you recognize it for the ridiculous and disrespectful behavior that it is? We will get to the chapters that give you the tools to create appropriate responses to customers who behave like this. For now I'd like you to be aware of what a disempowering word or phrase looks, sounds and feels like.

I am concentrating on "the customer is always right" because, like so many disempowering statements, it comes disguised as something that makes sense. On the surface it seems like an empowering rule to live by. However empowering and disempowering are opposites. An empowering word or phrase strengthens supports and encourages. It creates a positive environment of productivity and creative problem-solving. A disempowering word or phrase causes doubt and insecurity. It elicits defensive behavior.

"Always" is an absolute. The opposite of always right is always wrong, or never right. If the customer is *always right*, then the customer service rep, the salesperson, the technician and the business owner *must always be wrong*. Wow. What a great feeling. Why bother being in business at all if you're always wrong? That may seem extreme, however that is exactly what that *old saying* means. You may interpret it differently, yet this is my point: Why waste time and energy interpreting something when better word choices will make what you mean perfectly clear the first time you say it – without interpretation?

When you repeat "the customer is always right" in front of your employees, your message is disempowering. You are telling them, essentially, if there is ever a disagreement, a confrontation, or a case of

Section 2

he said/she said, then you will take your customer's side and your employee will be on his own. It also sets up "sides" where there is no need for any; you're all in it for a successful exchange of goods and services, right?

The theory the customer is always right is full of holes, and frankly, a statement like that puts you and your business at a disadvantage. There's no way you could live up to that standard; it is an absolute, which means it allows for no flexibility, special circumstances, human error, mistakes or miscommunication. When you fail or fall short – which is inevitable – you will feel discouraged and like a failure, and will look for someone or something to blame, causing unnecessary stress for yourself and your employees.

The saying, "the customer is always right," lands squarely in my column of disempowering words and phrases. What puts it there is the word *"always."* Always is an interesting word. You may believe it has the potential to be a force for good, carries a positive message or represents a strong desire to be the best you can be, as in: "We will always be there for you," "We always have the best prices," or "We always get it there on time." However, "always" is a definite, definable state of existence in space and time. It means "all ways," "in every way," "at all times," "in every shape and form" – without exception. In human reality, exceptions are the norm. To claim an "always" is to tell a lie.

You may have heard a few of the following comments from frustrated customers. How does it feel when a customer makes a blanket statement with the absolute "always" in it?

- "You always give me the run-around"
- "You guys always make me wait"
- "You're always late with your deliveries"
- "You always screw up my order somehow"
- "It always ends up more expensive than you said it would be"

Exceptional Care for Your Valued Client

Then there are the "nevers"; they go hand-in-hand with the "always" claim. While "always" means "all ways," "never" means "in no way," "at no point in time," "in no shape or form" – without exception. Also ridiculous, it might show up in comments like this:

- "You never return my phone calls"
- "You never show up on time"
- "You never come through on your promises"
- "You never get my order right"
- "No one in your company ever gives me a straight answer"

I have no patience for "shoulds" and absolutes; and it's challenging to be patient with those who use them chronically. These statements are designed to put you on the defensive, and in a catch-22. If you say nothing, you comply with the claim that you "always" fail in that area, with each and every customer you have had, do have, and will have. If you deny the claim, you look like an incompetent jerk that is too busy being defensive to resolve the situation.

Make no mistake: The use of "shoulds" and absolutes in the above examples are expressions of frustration, and indicate room for improvement in your business; they need to be taken seriously. Part of learning how to communicate with your customers is learning how to listen, how to reinterpret the "shoulds" and absolutes dispassionately, and how to regain control of the conversation so that it will become productive and useful.

Customers will use poor word choice now and then, and it will be up to you to recognize it for what it is in order to prevent it from scuttling or derailing what could be a profitable and productive business arrangement.

Avoid using *"should," "always," "never"* and other absolutes when you make claims about yourself, your business, your customers or your employees, especially when engaged in a customer service exchange.

Section 2

These are disempowering words. They criticize unfairly, whether obvious or implied, as with "should". When you hear a customer use a "should" or absolute, reframe their message back to them with more effective word choice.

"You should be able to tell me what's wrong over the phone. Can't you just tell me what's wrong with the pipes and what to do about it without coming out here? There can't be too many different things that can happen with plumbing. You should know what it's going to cost before you come to my house."

"It would certainly make my life easier if that were the case, I agree. However, what if I misunderstand you and charge for what I think it is, based on what you tell me, and start pulling things apart, and it turns out to be something different? It would be too bad to have to charge you for a mistake that could have been avoided with my personal inspection."

Going back to "*The customer is always right*," now that I've shown you why it's untrue and explained the role the "*always*" plays in making it an impossibility, I'm going to use this classic phrase to demonstrate the importance of saying what you mean, and saying it clearly so there is no room for doubt.

Begin with intention. The intention behind this phrase is to do what? Well, I believe its intention is actually good, that it is intended to serve as a reminder of how to treat a customer extraordinarily well, or as I like to say, provide exceptional care for your valued client. What are the reminders, specifically? Let's start a list:

1. To treat the customer with respect.
2. To listen to the customer attentively.
3. To empathize with the customer's point of view.
4. To be flexible or adaptable whenever possible; to bend over backwards to accommodate her needs.
5. To provide the kind of service that makes the customer feel like a VIP.

Exceptional Care for Your Valued Client

6. To demonstrate respect for the customer's intelligence.
7. To register the customer's concerns as legitimate, important, and deserving of attention.
8. To meet the customer's needs to the best of your ability.
9. To err on the side of the customer in the case of a misunderstanding whenever possible.
10. To make the extra effort to rise to the level of the customer's expectations, even if his standards are higher or more exacting than other customers', whenever possible.

Feel free to expand on this list. I would like to point out, though, that in my belief system each of the reminders simply elaborates on the first one: Treat the customer with respect. I call this behavior "Respectful Elegance," which I discuss in depth in an upcoming chapter.

The challenge with saying "The customer is always right" is some customers treat it as an excuse to behave like a bully. If you conduct your business by consistently and conscientiously treating your customers with respect, then aggressive behavior from one of them can be extremely challenging to deal with. Your front-line employees who have to bear the brunt of this behavior will be much more successful in their roles if they have a proper understanding of what this idea means to you in practical terms.

When you provide your definition of this phrase in a reframed statement designed to clearly express your priorities for customer service, you empower your employees to know which direction to take when someone tooting that horn comes into their space.

"Due to the delicate nature of our business, our policy is that front-office employees have no access to information beyond appointment windows for each specific agent. Rearranging schedules or changing appointments can only be done after you have confirmed the need with and obtained permission from the agent in question. You may explain the typical process each case goes through, step by step, and you may explain to a client where his or her specific case is in this process. Giving

Section 2

out any other information or answering any other questions about clients, cases generally or specifically, the nature of a case or even the workload involved on a case is forbidden. Senior executives are the only members of this staff who have the ability to judge whether information is sensitive and eyes-only, or can be made public in any form or arena."

Tony was a big fan of hard-boiled gum-shoe novels, so when he found himself accepting a position at what was essentially a detective agency and agreeing to adhere to this strict policy, he imagined he would soon be embroiled in the world of celebrity scandal, mixing it up with the seedy underbelly of society, and serving as the champion of long-legged dames in distress.

Instead, he found himself parked at a desk in the reception lobby from 8 a.m. to 5 p.m., answering phone calls and making appointments for the group of shirts-and-ties who spent most of their time researching the mundane on standard-issue computers, behind standard-issue cubicle walls, eating standard-issue sandwiches at their desks and discussing standard-issue 30-something topics like whose kid was playing soccer and whose mother-in-law was in town for the weekend. No guns, no stake-outs, no glitz or glamour – it was nothing like the books he'd read.

Yet he knew he played an important role in protecting clients and keeping their secrets. While he had no access to those secrets, he was the gatekeeper that prevented anyone else from taking even the first step towards getting their hands on sensitive files or damaging documents.

He was the first impression, the first line of defense. New clients walked in, unsure of what to expect, nervous, maybe embarrassed, and it was up to Tony to put them at ease, educate them about the process, match them with an appropriate agent, set up a consultation or follow-up appointment and put them at ease. He was the first brick in the foundation of trust the agency would build with each new client.

His job was to be friendly, knowledgeable, approachable, firm but pleasant. Tony had mere moments, whether on the phone or in the

Exceptional Care for Your Valued Client

lobby, to convey confidence, competence and a talent for discretion. He did his job very well.

Most clients were reassured by the presence of the efficient gatekeeper, but Marcia Stone was no ordinary client. Marcia had trouble giving up control. She needed the services of a professional investigator, but she wanted to make sure her case was handled according to her definition of how it "should" be managed. She had a lot of questions and tried to make a lot of demands.

"I should be able to talk to my agent whenever I want. He works for me," Marcia said angrily when she walked off the street one afternoon without an appointment.

"I'm sorry he's unavailable right now, and I do know he spent the morning focusing on your case and assigned an extra person to track down a new lead," Tony replied.

"What new lead? He should have called me right away."

"I understand we have your permission to look into new leads as they come up, and in the interest of efficiency we investigate and then report findings," Tony said in a friendly and engaging tone. "We know how hard it is to wait for updates and how disappointing it can be when we tell you about a lead and it ends up going nowhere. If it turns out to be important, he will call you as soon as possible, otherwise he will include it in your meeting on Monday. His team is very discreet, so that's all I know."

"Well, I want to see him before Monday. While I'm here I want to move that meeting up to Thursday."

"Okay, I will put in a request right away to reschedule and call you personally as soon as he confirms it," Tony said, turning to his keyboard to enter the request.

"When I need to reschedule an appointment, I shouldn't have to wait for

Section 2

you to call back. Just look at his schedule and tell me when he can see me," Marcia bridled. "This is ridiculous. What is wrong with you people?"

"I understand that you're frustrated. It seems like an easy thing to do, however with so many people on each team it's really in your best interest and in the interests of our other clients to make sure we coordinate our schedules and get permission before making any changes. I will have an answer for you before 2 p.m. if that's helpful," Tony offered.

"When you were dying to get me in here as a new client there was no hassle with getting 'permission' to make an appointment," Marcia sneered.

One of the senior managers appeared in a doorway. Tony began to feel rattled. Had he said or done something wrong? He took a deep breath, and even though he knew she had already been given all this information he decided that taking offense would only make things worse. Instead, he chose to remind her politely that they were providing great service.

"You're right," he said. "It is easier to make an appointment for a new client than for an existing one. There's very little preparation that goes into the first meeting, compared with the work that it takes to prepare for an update meeting. We want to make sure the time you spend down here in the building has as much value as possible for you."

Marcia sniffed. He made sense. "I guess I can wait for your call. But can you do me a favor?"

"Of course."

"Can you ask him if he thinks it's better for me to wait until Monday, if he'll have more to tell me, or if Thursday is a good idea? It's just so hard to wait."

Tony nodded, "I know. If you can wait, I do know that a couple of days can make a difference, especially at this stage in the case. This is typically how it works."

Exceptional Care for Your Valued Client

As the gatekeeper, Tony understood his limitations. He could tell that his inability to change appointments without making her wait for a phone call, answer her questions or acquiesce to her demands – or even reassure her in the positive that someone else could acquiesce to them – was extremely frustrating for her. Fortunately, he also understood enough about the logic and process behind the way he had to handle clients that he was empowered to choose the words that would satisfy her.

After Marcia left, the senior manager stepped out of his doorway and approached Tony, giving him a pat on the back.

"I like the way you handled that, Tony," he said. "You said all the right things. Some clients find it hard to be patient. I want you to know that if you have a difficult person out here and need help, you can call one of us to back you up. Good job."

It is of the utmost importance that your employees feel empowered, especially when dealing with challenging customers. Feeling empowered is what enables them to deal with challenges in the first place. It comes from understanding the scope of both their responsibilities and limitations, understanding what is expected of them when they're working with a customer on their own, understanding how your operation works, and of course, understanding that you will back them up when they make an effort to clarify information for a customer or bend over backwards to accommodate him.

Empowering others requires a conscious effort. So does identifying and eliminating the words and phrases that are disempowering. If you have had any success untying the (k)nots and exterminating members of the Hit List Six from your vocabulary, than you are going to really enjoy and appreciate the way getting rid of the absolutes I tackle, in the next chapter, can change your life. One friend has taken so strongly to the understanding of how damaging absolutes can be that she has gone beyond disallowing them at work; she refuses to let her children use them at home.

Section 2

Chapter 9

Shoulds, Absolutes, and More Words to Watch Out For

"Shoulds" and absolutes, like *"all," "nothing," "every"* and *"never,"* do you, and your listener a disservice. When you choose to use these words you run the very serious risk of coming across as an exaggerator, an aggressor and an unreasonable person. Equally damaging are the vague phrases like "no problem" and "no worries"; these are the indicators you have no idea what you're talking about, that you have something to hide, or you're unreliable.

Here are yet more powerful arguments for choosing to speak your message clearly, precisely, and accurately.

"Should" is a horrible word of unrealistic expectation, often in retrospect, when it's too late to do anything about it (you shouldn't have done that), and failure (it should have been done differently).

Here's the thing about "should": Whatever happened should have happened, otherwise something else would have happened.

There's no way around a "should;" it's a statement of facts in existence. This is one time I will use an absolute, and appropriately so: Everything that has happened should have happened; because it happened – regardless of your feelings about it. This is the "scientific should."

Take as long as you need to think that through in order to understand its truth.

Saying an event "shouldn't have happened" the way it did, or even that it "should have happened differently" is pointless and disempowering. People make decisions and take action based on the information they have in front of them. If that information or their interpretation of it was at fault, address that fact appropriately with an eye to "next time" and use it as a positive, empowering teaching opportunity.

Exceptional Care for Your Valued Client

Reflecting on an error or mishap can bring up the impulse to say how things "should" or "should not" have been handled.

"You should know better! You should have done this! You should have done that! You shouldn't have done it that way!"

You may think that's a constructive way to prevent a repeat, however there are much better ways to approach analyzing the situation. Of course you want to determine where words and actions stopped being effective. Here is where you have to take a deep breath and make a decision. Do you want to empower the people involved to learn, grow and succeed? Or do you want to punish, point fingers, and strip them of a sense of worth, intelligence and power; so in the future they will be unsure of themselves, less confident about their ability to deliver the goods and services the way you want, and less than enthusiastic about representing you well to your customers.

That is what disempowering words and phrases do. Direct them at your employees and your employees lose faith in themselves and you. Direct them at your customers and your customers lose faith in you.

- "It should be done this afternoon." Is that supposed to be a commitment?
- "It should work just fine now." Is this supposed to garner confidence in your abilities?
- "It shouldn't be a problem." But what if it is?

I feel anxious when I hear this kind of "reassurance" from someone I'm trusting to take care of my needs, whether it's repair work or placing a special order.

You know the negative feelings that come up when you get *"should on"* by customers, and there's a whole set of skills necessary to respond effectively to an aggressive "should-er" so you can navigate out of the state of defensiveness they put you in. Knowing that it takes extra effort

Section 2

and special knowledge to deal effectively with someone who uses disempowering words and phrases, do you want to put your customers in a position where they feel they have to defend themselves to you, where they have to start using special skills in order to sift through what you're saying?

Take a moment to think about how "shoulds" show up when you're talking to your customers. Have you been guilty of any version of the following? How do you think your customers appreciate being "should" on?

"Silly girl, you should have come to see me sooner; I should be the only one who knows you're going gray."

"Now, now, Mrs. Jones, you know you shouldn't turn your back on that kid for a minute. I mean really, what's he going to put in the DVD player next time?"

"Tom – again? You should learn how to park better or we're going to get rich off beating dents out of your bumpers."

Even if you think you're just engaging in friendly teasing, "shoulding" on a customer is insulting. My colleague LuAnn Buechler will be delving into the art of "taking friendly banter too far" in a later chapter. For now, consider whether you may be falling into that danger zone.

Slipping into an absolute is as easy as slipping into a *"should."* They may seem harmless, as in "I always exaggerate, it's just who I am. Everyone knows what I really mean." They sure do. They know better than to rely on you for correct information. You may think absolutes merely underline what you're saying, but you're wrong. They have an emotional impact, and it's usually bad.

Absolutes have no place in reality, unless you're talking about math. Two plus two will always equal four. Great. Granted. Two plus two will never equal three. Fine. Accepted. When it comes to human reality, especially performance reality, absolutes are just plain inaccurate.

Exceptional Care for Your Valued Client

"We always answer the phone on the second ring." Is that a goal or a reflection of reality? Stated like this, it's a claim about reality. Is it conceivable that a salesperson who already had her hand poised to dial the phone might hear it ring and lift the receiver on the first ring as a reflex? How about those times when you're short of staff, all three people are already talking to customers, and it takes more than two rings to excuse themselves and reach over to get the phone?

"Always" is an absolute. So is "never." Other absolutes include the blanket claims that begin with "every" and "all." Here are some common examples:

Every day	All week
Every time	All the time
Everyone	All your co-workers
Everyone else	All your competitors
Every customer	All your customers

Unless you can prove otherwise, these words are lies.

In the first few chapters my purpose was to persuade you; when it comes to client service, your communication skills and the communication skills of those you employ to represent you can make or break your business. I introduced the concept of simple word choice as a powerful tool that can strengthen those skills, and in turn, raise the standard of exceptional care you deliver. Beginning with the why and the how of untying (k)nots in your speech, I introduced the first step toward reframing your customer service "speak," and gave you some real-world exercises to begin playing with.

Now that you are aware learning to communicate is like learning to do anything else; and there is a Process of Re-Education to go through on this journey, I hope you are having fun with the state of hyper-awareness you may find yourself in whenever you open your mouth.

I have targeted and shared with you the most important words that need to be eliminated from your vocabulary so you can make room for

Section 2

stronger, clearer, more empowering words to take their places. Avoiding the confusing and disempowering words and choices is one thing, and deciding what to replace them with requires you to pay attention to rebuilding your sentence as you speak it.

In order to achieve effective communication you must figure out how to say what you want to say clearly. A clear statement holds its own power. A clear statement is empowering for each person involved in the exchange. Confusion undermines that power, therefore, anything less than a clear statement robs you of your power to get your message across.

While I'm on this subject, I want to remind you of how tying your sentence up with a (k)not twists it up so the customer's brain registers the opposite information, and then detangles your message. Remembering that "Don't forget" registers first as "forget," "I can't help it" registers as "I can help it," and "it's (k)not easy" registers as "it's easy," I want to draw your attention to a couple of commonly used expressions that are supposed to garner confidence., but do the opposite.

I hear people telling their customers "no worries" and "no problem" and I cringe. Why on earth would you want to put the words "worries" and "problem" in someone's head? Is it so they can associate worrying and problems with doing business with you? Leave those words out of it! Keep them out of your mouth, out of the air, out of their ears, out of their heads!

Instead of trying to reassure your customer with "no worries" or "no problem," be clear and forthright. Choose one of these for example:

Customer: "Can you arrange that for me?"

Friendly response that has your customer thinking there is something to worry about: "No worries"

Friendly response that really does reassure your customer: "Of course" or "Happy to"

Exceptional Care for Your Valued Client

Customer: "I appreciate what you are doing for me"

Friendly answer that has your customer thinking it really is a problem: "No problem"

Friendly response that really does reassure your customer: "My pleasure" or "Our pleasure

Worry-free, problem-free, hassle-free. They're all cute little ways of trying to say "trust us, we know what we're doing, our system is streamlined for your ease of mind." What they do, though, is create anxiety in your customer. For example, the word "hassle" stresses out my friend. She immediately imagines herself at the end of a long line at the Department of Motor Vehicles, where she once spent three hours getting her car registered in a new state. Tell her the process is smooth and she'll go for it. Bring up the word "hassle," even with that "-free" behind it, and she avoids whatever is being offered.

Affirm your strengths with clear and positive language. Adding "no" before a negative, disempowering word like "worries" or "problem" backfires; it just introduces the negative to the experience. Adding "-free" to the back of a negative, disempowering word fails to cancel out the negative impact of the disempowering word. I know what you're trying to do: The intention is to highlight that what you offer is something free of worries, problems and hassles. So say what it is you are offering, and be confident enough to trust in the power of that clear statement.

If you're tempted to use a cute but ironically negative word like "stress-free" to describe something you have to offer your customer, use one of these instead:

Easy	Efficient
Fast	Slow
Streamlined	Comprehensive
Prompt	Private

Section 2

Describe your strengths for what they are. Describe them for what they are "(k)not" will backfire. Be proud of what you have to offer, and make sure you express them with confidence. That's empowering.

Large	Award-winning
Small	Established
Plentiful	Old-fashioned
Strong	Cutting edge
Subtle	Hand-made
Advanced	Machine-tooled

In customer service exchanges, teach yourself to drop the disempowering words. Remember that "shoulds" and absolutes set you up for failure. Since you are working toward being an Exceptional Care provider, get rid of them now and choose to be clear, positive and empowering. Affirm what you have to offer without stooping to throwaway phrases that do no one a service.

Drop them from your vocabulary. Choose to speak clearly; refuse to rely on words that are vague or open for misinterpretation. I suggest substituting these phrases until you get more comfortable coming up with your own:

"A technician should call you back in a few minutes" – *"I'm going to ask the first available technician to call you."*

"It should be ready for you by this afternoon" – *"I estimate the job will be completed by 4 p.m. I will call you personally at 3:30 if it looks like it will take longer."*

"We always find the perfect dress for our brides" – *"We have had great success finding a beautiful dress for each of our brides in the past, and I'm excited to do the same for you. Would you like to read our customer reviews?"*

"We always use the best tools on the market" – *"We use the best tools available"*

Exceptional Care for Your Valued Client

"We never make you wait for an appointment" – *"We schedule our appointments to avoid overlaps and the inconvenience of delays."*

"We never duplicate orders" – *"We have a process in place that helps us avoid duplicating orders"*

Be clear when you make statements to your customers, and when she says "you said..." and quotes you, it will be okay to admit the customer is right. Test it out. Imagine a frustrated customer walks up to you and quotes the first example: "you said a technician would call me back in a few minutes" Uh-oh. "Should" got confused with "would" – it happens a lot. Look out now: It's time to back-pedal, explain yourself, apologize, swim in the deep end of defensiveness. Now imagine the same customer walks up to you and quotes the second example: "You said 'I'm going to ask the first available technician to call you.'" Regardless of how long it took for the technician to call, the information you gave the customer originally still holds up to scrutiny. Apologies may be in order if it took a long time, but there's no need for back-pedaling.

A disempowering word or statement puts you on the defensive. An empowering word or statement engenders a sense of confidence. In the event of a mishap or confrontation, a disempowering word or statement bogs you down in that defensive mode, whereas a sense of confidence enables you to progress past the apologies and right into resolving the issue at hand helpfully, cheerfully, and with the potential to turn a negative experience for the customer into a positive experience that is both impressive and memorable.

Creating powerful, empowering communication with your customers begins with word choice, and the standard for choosing the best words to do that job is what I talk about in the next chapter: *Respectful Elegance*.

Section 2

Chapter 10

Respectful Elegance via your Employees

"An indisputable business fact is that people do business with people they like. It makes sense, therefore, to like and be liked by as many people as possible. The ability to create rapport with a large number of people is a fundamental skill in sales, management, personal relationships, and everyday life".

"We have all heard of the Golden Rule and many people aspire to live by it. Do unto others as you would have them do unto you. The Golden Rule implies the basic assumption that other people would like to be treated the way that you would like to be treated. The alternative to the Golden Rule is much more productive. I call it the Platinum Rule: "Treat others the way they want to be treated. Ah hah! What a difference. The Platinum Rule accommodates the feelings of others."

Adapted from Dr. Tony Alassandra's book:
The Platinum Rule (Warner Books, 1996)

In the world of verbal and non-verbal communication (body language), Respectful Elegance is a powerful demonstration of the Platinum Rule. Treat others the way they want to be treated; or in other words: Speak to people the way they want to be spoken to. Communicate with people the way they want to be communicated with. In return they will be treating you, speaking to you and communicating with you the way you appreciate being treated, spoken to and communicated with.

I love this concept. It is so clear, and so obvious, and summarizes the "what and why" of my message beautifully.

Especially in challenging situations, like when I'm describing a complex idea, laying out an intricate plan, or steering a confrontation back to a conversation, I have the most success when I first check myself against the standard of Respectful Elegance.

Exceptional Care for Your Valued Client

"How can I best put this so that the other person understands what I'm saying? Which words will make it perfectly clear?" Choosing words that leave room for doubt, leave something out, contradict each other, or make your customer work too hard to understand demonstrates a lack of respect.

Respectful Elegance is taking into consideration what your communication looks and sounds like on the other end. Check yourself: Are you talking to hear yourself talk, to knock out the key points in your script as fast as possible, or to get this customer out of your hair so you can move on to the next one? What is the point of the string of words coming out of your mouth; what do you want them to do? Is your purpose to irritate and confuse your customer, or is it perhaps to educate, inform, persuade, confirm, connect or otherwise empower him to use you as a resource (and pay for the privilege)?

It may very well be, in your opinion, the information you have is basic and obvious. That's because you already have it. Customers who ask questions and/or are having a hard time understanding the subject matter need you to enlighten them. Be the hero. Explain politely and be patient, even if it's the 14th time you told a person that morning how many shots of espresso are in the 20 oz latte, or the 28th time you told someone that carpet samples are in the flooring department, or the 200th time you directed customers to take the second left past the railroad tracks instead of the first. Remember; the news is new to each new person.

It's your job to make your customer feel like you're kind-of glad they stopped you and asked for clarification, regardless of what you may think of what's being asked.

"That's a great question. A garlic press is indeed intended to crush garlic."

"Yes, you're right. You can park in our lot when you come here to shop."

Section 2

"I am happy to make sure your ocean-view room faces the water."

"Well, the 10-piece chicken meal has 10 pieces, and the 6-piece meal has six pieces, so yes, I think you're right; it sounds like the 10-piece meal will feed more people."

"No, there's no need for us to contract out to someone else to make the beer. Since we are a brewery we have all the equipment we need right here."

Can I crush garlic in a garlic press? Can I park in your parking lot? Does an ocean-view room face the water? Will a 10-piece or 6-piece meal feed more people? Who makes the beer for your brewery? Are you kidding me? Exceptional Care is about being friendly, helpful and efficient even while you're wondering if the customer left his ability to think on his pillow that morning.

By its very nature, being in the process of providing exceptional care for your valued client means being "on" every moment there's a customer in range, regardless of how tired, bored, or close to the end of the shift you're getting.

Several years ago, I owned an ice cream shop in Springfield, Illinois. It was a fun place with a great crew. The young people who worked for me were friendly, cheerful, worked quickly, had a great rapport with each other, liked what they were doing, and enjoyed dishing out ice cream. They kept the containers well-stocked, the counters clean, the music light and the laughter ready. I had a really fantastic team working for me.

After a month or two of being in business, when the newness had settled into a rhythm, I started to notice a strange phenomenon. It seemed my staff worked best and gave the highest quality of exceptional care when the place was packed and the pressure was on, and they could have been excused for slipping.

They kept the energy level up, made eye contact, gave out huge happy smiles, got complicated orders right just about every time, and had

Exceptional Care for Your Valued Client

endless patience with those special customers who, like many of us, would find it almost physically painful to have to decide between ice cream flavors.

To a person, my staff remembered details like how big a scoop of nuts went on which sundae, in what order to build a layered dessert, how to hand a cone over with enough napkins, and how to up-sell or mention a special promotion. They were on top of their game.

However, when business was at a slower pace and customers walked in at random intervals, my people would slip. They would take a little longer to scoop the ice cream, continue to chat with a co-worker, forget the customer asked to leave the nuts off, or fidget if someone was taking a while to make up their mind.

Here's why. When customers are in front of you, one after the other, you are tuned in to that process, and all the details required to serve and sell to that person are in the forefront of your mind and waiting on your tongue. You're using the same skills and words repeatedly, and they are part of your groove. Take the customer away long enough to interrupt that rhythm, then bring him back later, and getting back into the groove can take a minute.

As asked, my employees were finding other ways to occupy themselves in the downtime between rushes. The customer who walked in during those periods got divided attention by default. They became the interruption of work rather than the purpose. I dealt with this dilemma by constantly reminding my employees to adjust their posture or voice as soon as that customer walked through the door. A conscious and deliberate change in movement and vocal attitude would trigger a shift in their focus and energy level. They were turning themselves back "on."

By changing their physiology, which is a subject I tackle in section three, they could snap out of one role and into another. Yet it had to be a conscious effort. Respectful Elegance demands that effort be made.

The other phenomenon that struck me as counter-productive was the

Section 2

closing-time ritual and what it did psychologically to my employees. In food service, closing the shop for the night includes a series of take-down chores that go beyond just turning things off; equipment has to be cleaned, surfaces wiped down and scrubbed, chairs put on tables, floors mopped, and a slew of other time consuming tasks needing to be done after the last order has come in.

What I found was happening on slow nights was by general consensus my staff was starting the take-down ritual early in order to get out and on their way as close to closing time as possible. That would have been okay, except when a customer wandered in somewhere between 10 and two minutes before closing time.

If the food and/or equipment is put away when your customer walks in you either turn him away and risk never seeing him again, or you reverse the work you just did and get things rolling again to take care of his needs. In that case, the customer is more than an interruption; he's an object of resentment.

When I published my hours by painting them on the front door and listing them on advertising fliers and business cards, I made a contract with my customers that I would sell them my products promptly at opening time and right through to closing time. Nowhere in any of my advertising did I say closing time was 10 minutes to something. It was my responsibility to make good on that promise, without fail.

When my employees began the closing ritual, even if they left enough product ready for last-minute customers, it triggered a change in attitude and energy level away from customer service mode and over to "the day is done; I'm getting out of here" mode. I effectively lost productivity the minute they started in on that first closing task.

The best way to handle this dilemma was to decide, as the owner, that paying them to stay and complete take-down chores after closing was more profitable than letting them start closing early so they would be off the clock sooner. I made the decision to budget for that extra payroll time after the doors were locked. It was better than having a customer

Exceptional Care for Your Valued Client

spread the word that they had been turned away with time still left on my contract with him.

You know what? My staff, being eager to get home, worked more quickly and efficiently, and paid better attention to detail after we were closed, and subsequently cost me less than I had anticipated.

As an employer or manager, you can safe-guard the *Respectful Elegance* your staff conveys by paying attention to the things that erode it, and then work diligently to avoid those pitfalls.

Think of your employees as your internal customers. Treat your employees the way they want to be treated: with respect. Instill in them the initiative to treat customers the way they would like to be treated and they will be loyal, returning clients. There's that Platinum Rule again. If you tend to be dismissive, or listen without looking at them, or fail to follow through to make sure information makes sense, then that's how they will treat the people who come to do business with you.

Be aware of the constraints you put on your employees and the effects they have on customer service exchanges. If you push them to wrap up an interaction too soon or move too quickly from one customer to the next, they will speed up their speech. They will take the cue from you that customers are unworthy of time, patience, and respect.

Talking too fast is offensive. It is as bad as talking with food in your mouth. I really hope you had a physical reaction to the thought of talking to a customer with food in your mouth; that is so far beneath *Respectful Elegance* that it hits the floor and keeps burrowing south past lack of respect, past downright disrespectful, and straight into the realm of *cussing at a customer*. Trust me, it's bad.

Back to talking too fast. It is one of the best and clearest ways to tell a customer that you have no interest in them, their needs, or their business. "Hey there, customer!" you're saying. "You really are just another number. Can you tell how much we care about your business?"

Section 2

When you rush your exceptional care message, you alienate your customer. Rushing your customer cuts off his access to your product or service; it shuts him down. It builds a wall between him and what you have to offer. I'm betting you've had a few of those calls where the person on the other end of the line is clearly bored, clearly reading from a script for the umpteen millionth time that day, and clearly wants to get the whole call over with as fast as possible.

When I get a phone call from a rushed individual I wonder if that business has any clue they are squandering the access route to their product or service. I respond in kind: I find myself in a rush to get rid of them.

Your employees' communication skill-set is your customers' access route to your product or service. Remember Tony and his role as gatekeeper and first-impression-maker at the detective agency? Your customer has to go through your employee to get to your goods. When you and your employees fail to communicate clearly, you become your biggest obstacle. And only you can shift the paradigm. Keep that access route open, and keep it as clear and easy to follow as possible, and your customers will find their way back to you time and again.

Let's go back to an example of "shoulding" I showed you in the last chapter and explore how to apply *Respectful Elegance* to the situation.

The temptation is to say, "You should know better! You should have done this! You should have done that! You shouldn't have done it that way!" But where does this get you? You could be more specific:

"You should have checked everything better! You shouldn't have assumed any of it was accurate! Customers never know what they're talking about. Look what happened – everything after that point was wrong and it all got screwed up! What a waste of time and money. We look like complete idiots!

"But again, where does this get you?

Exceptional Care for Your Valued Client

How does that kind of rant teach an employee to handle the task successfully the next time it comes across his desk? Where in there did you take the time to reinforce the right way to do it?

"From now on, I need you to verify all of the data personally, even if it seems trivial, before moving on to the next step. Remember that getting the information can be very confusing for customers, so relying on them to look it up for you is a bad idea. You are responsible for making sure every digit and every detail is correct. When we do it right the first time, we make money and more importantly, me make the customer happy. Cutting corners costs us money and reputation. Is there anything about the process that is unclear to you? I would be happy to spend some time going over it with you."

Three things accomplished: You reinforced your expectations, re-explained why it needs to be done your way, and opened the door for your employee to ask for help. That's another demonstration of Respectful Elegance.

How have you empowered your employees today? Do they understand what is expected of them? Do they have all the information at their fingertips, and do they know how to use it and interpret it well enough to pass it on? Have you demonstrated what it looks like?

A good way to explain it is by highlighting some of its opposites. Think of them as "turn offs." Being "should" on is a turn off. Talking with your mouth full is a turn off. Talking too fast to get all the words out in a rush is a turn off. Making it painfully obvious you are bored is a turn off. Making it obvious that you think your customer is too dumb to walk and chew gum at the same time is a definite turn off.

Do you recognize any of these traits in your team? What have you done to empower them to behave differently? Again: Have you demonstrated what Respectful Elegance looks like? Have you set up your business policies to support their ability and desire to behave with Respectful Elegance? If they are young and inexperienced, have you approached them honestly and made it clear – respectfully – that they are to change

Section 2

their behavior, and how they are to do it? Following through with all of the above is Respectful Elegance in action. It's empowering.

Can you imagine what a great feeling it will be when you can trust your employees to treat your customers with Exceptional Care even when you're nowhere near the building? By showing them what Respectful Elegance looks and sounds like, you will be able to serve as a role model. By recognizing it when it happens, and applying some positive reinforcement (another act of Respectful Elegance) you will be able to continue to empower them and reap the benefits.

Exceptional Care for Your Valued Client

Section 2

Chapter 11

Respectful Elegance and the Power of Self-Esteem

You know you're using Respectful Elegance when your client feels good about herself, capable of following along with what you're saying, competent enough to make good decisions, and that she's engaging enough to hold your attention during a conversation, even if she's just buying the gum she's going to walk away chewing on.

This requires patience, especially when you are explaining a complicated process. It requires the ability and desire to break down a complex set of ideas or instructions into a basic string of logic that anyone can follow, without coming across as condescending.

Most importantly, it requires clear and direct language.

Clarity is the greatest way to show respect for your customer. Keep the (k)nots and No's and vague language out of there. Regardless of whether you believe the information will be received as good news or bad news, respectful elegance requires you tell it like it is, graciously and with the expectation your customer has the intelligence and character to appreciate being treated like an adult. If he falls short of your expectation, that's on him. We'll talk about how to deal with that in the next chapter. LuAnn has years of experience in that field; she's had to work with all kinds of people in countless different high-stress, fast-paced scenarios.

When you look and sound like you are paying attention, genuinely care, are fully engaged, and that the person in front of you is your top priority, you are demonstrating Respectful Elegance. When you listen attentively, without pre-conceived ideas, and really tune in to what your client is saying, it empowers you to speak clearly, respond clearly and to deliver your information without creating confusion. This in turn empowers your client and creates a solid foundation of trust and loyalty. You become their go-to-guy (or gal) for the product or service you're

Exceptional Care for Your Valued Client

providing. Your client knows that he can come to you for what he needs, that you can be counted on to break the process down into clear, efficient and straightforward chunks of information for him, and that when he leaves your business he will feel less like a dope who is in over his head and more like a competent adult who has the situation under control.

If you have done your job right and employed Respectful Elegance with your customer, then he will feel like the smartest guy on the block because he took his needs to the right person. He will leave the work in your competent hands, and yet feel securely in control.

Respectful Elegance is lacking when your customer feels "talked down to," rushed, ridiculed, like an idiot, or disempowered in any other way. If your customer walks away feeling any kind of doubt in his decision-making abilities, he will doubt the wisdom of coming to you. If your competitor makes him feel like he's smart, that's where he'll take his business.

Being able to make a client feel that his decision to go to you is a good reflection on him, that it means he's smart, wise, discerning, able to make good decisions, and that he's in control is important. Would you like to guess what else brings a customer back? Feeling attractive.

"Bob!" you say, "I refuse to flirt with my customers! Gross!"

Relax. I am in no way suggesting that you flirt with a customer, hit on him, or hand your phone number over with a wink to secure an up-sell. I'm talking about the little things other people do when they talk to us that make us feel good about ourselves. Eye contact. A smile that reaches the eyes. A sign of recognition when we walk in. A little bit of small talk, and some kind of comment that is unique to the exchange, even if it's obvious that a customer service script is in use. Evidence that the client matters is important. Feeling attractive and memorable is part of that.

Subtlety and normality are key here. Overtly making someone feel attractive can be pretty creepy, unless you're selling beauty or beautiful adornments and your understood purpose is to make your customer feel exceptionally beautiful.

Section 2

Few people want to do business with someone who gives off a "creepy vibe," so I discourage trying too hard. A creepy vibe emanates from someone whose compliments, expression or look in his eyes are incongruent with the rest of his communication style. It just feels "off." Human beings pick up on that sort of thing and distrust the flatterer.

Oh sure, sometimes it can be exciting and put a bounce in your step, but that feeling is easily replaced by a feeling of foolishness; you start to feel like a fool for falling for something so cheap and transparent in the first place. It's a very bad idea to put your customers in that position. That's why it's called "unprofessional."

What I do encourage you to do is understand what the absence of these cues of attractiveness do to your customer psychologically. The absence of eye contact and a smile screams "you are too ugly to look at" or at the very least, makes them self-conscious. Most people walk around with some kind of insecurity going on in their heads. One customer may think she's having a bad hair day, or that she is underdressed, or even that her sunglasses left crooked indentations on the bridge of her nose. Another customer may be wondering if the stain on his tie is obvious, or worried about the dampness he can feel in his armpits.

When you fail to give those subtle signals that reassure him he's welcome in your establishment, that void may very well be filled with self-doubt and insecurity. When that happens, your customer will begin to associate your business with negative feelings, and off he will go to somewhere they smile at him.

The lack of friendly cues that signal interest in making a connection makes us feel invisible. It makes us feel ignored even when we're being served. Oddly enough, it is the customer's right to ignore you when you drop the soda off at his table; however, ignoring him when you drop the soda off at his table is unbelievably rude.

There is no way to tell, just by looking at a person, whether they have insecurities – let alone what they are. When I worked for the Alaska Wild, an Indoor Football League team in Anchorage, Alaska, the average age of

Exceptional Care for Your Valued Client

the cheerleaders who performed at the games was 19. They were young, beautiful, talented, kind and intelligent – the whole package. One of the sponsors donated hair and make-up services, and another donated gym memberships, so it would be safe to assume they had every reason to feel confident and beautiful at all times. I was surprised to learn that any of these women could have had a single insecurity. And yet, each one had her own secret fear that some flaw only she could identify was somehow obvious to everyone she met. My point is; even the most attractive of us needs reassurance we're worth the time it takes to smile.

My point is; even the most attractive of us needs to be reassured that we're worth the time it takes to smile.

The eye contact, smiling and small talk may go unnoticed by the average customer. Polite behavior is accepted as the norm, and rightly so. But the lack thereof will almost always be taken as an affront. In other words, it goes unnoticed until it fails to show up – and then it really gets noticed.

"Their product is okay, but their service is very poor." Being known for having a great product yet mediocre service is worse than being known for having great service and a mediocre product. Take a look at what I found at www.customerservicemanager.com under "facts & figures":

- 56%-70% of the customers who complain to you will do business with you again if you resolve their problem. If they feel you acted quickly and to their satisfaction, up to 96% will do business with you again, and they will probably refer other people to you. Source: the White House Office of Consumer Affairs, Washington, DC.

- A dissatisfied customer will tell 9-15 people about it. And approximately 13% of your dissatisfied customers will tell more than 20 people about their problem. Source: the White House Office of Consumer Affairs, Washington, DC.

- Happy customers who have their problems resolved will tell 4-6 people about their positive experience. Source: the White House Office of Consumer Affairs, Washington, DC.

Section 2

- The average "wronged customer" will tell 8-16 people about it. Over 20% will tell more than 20. Source: Lee Resource Inc.

- 91% of unhappy customers will not willingly do business with you again. Source: Lee Resource Inc.

- 70% of complaining customers will do business with you again if you resolve the complaint in their favour. Source: Lee Resource Inc.

- 95% of complaining customers will do business with you again if you resolve the complaint instantly. Source: Lee Resource Inc.

- 80% of complaints received by an organization are likely to have poor communication as their root cause, either with the customer or within the organization itself. Source: Unknown.

These are all powerful statistics that help illustrate the importance of paying attention to your customers and making sure you employ Respectful Elegance in your communication with them at all times. The more developed your communication skills are, the more receptive you are to what your valued clients are telling you, which means the more likely they are to bring issues to your attention, and the more likely they are to give you a chance to resolve them before emotions get involved.

Providing Exceptional Care for your valued client includes creating a comfort level that includes knowing they can come to you with honest feedback, even when it is less than glowing.

How many of us keep returning to a restaurant with decent but "nothing to write home about" food because we enjoy how we're received and treated while we're there? If a meal is "to die for" but the server barely acknowledges our presence, is that meal enough to bring you back when you're in the mood for an enjoyable dining experience?

Respectful Elegance is important. Are you ever too busy, too slammed, to pass a smile across the counter, or to say a full "thank you"? Seriously. If you're looking to save seconds, I hope you're prepared for

Exceptional Care for Your Valued Client

the cost. Are those seconds worth sending a customer down the street for more personal service? You can take a few heart beats to create a Signature Moment, no matter what else is going on. It may take some conscious effort at first, but will become second nature quickly. Your clients will notice and remark on it.

"Thank you" is a sign of respect. In the order of things, "thanks" is a throwaway term that lacks effort; the absence of an acknowledgement shows a lack of respect; and a sneer is disrespectful. Be better than all of these.

Respectful Elegance extends "thank you" to "thank you for coming to see us today," and "thank you for being on time," and "thank you for making a follow-up appointment."

Respectful Elegance has a twofold purpose. While you're busy treating your customer with respect, you're treating yourself the same way. Think about it. Speaking clearly the first time saves you from having to repeat yourself, or consult your mental thesaurus for a better way to say it. It's an insurance policy against claims that you misrepresented yourself. Most of all, it instills confidence in you the speaker. Being clear in word and message is empowering. There are no two ways about whatever you have said. You put it out there. When your customer accepts the unadorned as your word, and goes with it, that's empowering.

Pharmacists understand the importance of *R*Respectful Elegance. They know what's at stake if they fail to make sure the customer understands how to manage her prescription.

Is there anything more frustrating than bringing home a box containing build-it-yourself furniture, clearing space to put it together, gathering up the tools you will need and counting out the screws and nuts and bolts – only to realize later that the instructions are in another language or mix up steps, or a color is off or a diagram unclear?

Remember the old joke, told 1,000 different ways, where some unsuspecting driver pulls up to a couple of local characters to ask for directions and is given directions like, "Turn left where the Johnson barn

Section 2

burned down 15 years ago," "When you get to the fork in the road go right and you'll wind around a bit for about six or seven miles till you get to the river, but the bridge is out so don't go that way," and "Turn right about a mile or so before the railroad tracks."

How is anyone supposed to follow instructions when there is a big chunk of information are missing?

Recognizing the need for clarity when your customer is relying on you for information is an important first step. Achieving clarity takes some work. The pay-offs are big, though. The easier you make finding and using your goods and services, the more they will be sought after and used.

Here's a quick list of instances of opportunity where you can take advantage of what I'm laying out for you here, right now. Does your exceptional care include providing any of the following:

- Instructions
- Descriptions
- Directions
- Maps
- Plans
- Rules of conduct
- Expectations
- Guidelines
- Service plans
- Warranties
- "What to do in case of…"

Challenge yourself. Select one of the above that you employ in your exceptional care routine. It could be something basic like giving directions over the phone, or something complex like outlining a legal process. Sit down with it and imagine yourself completely ignorant of the first step. Read the first step out loud: Would it make sense to a foreigner? Does it assume your customer's starting point is further along than the beginning? "Once the desk has been assembled, begin putting the hutch together" forgets an important step: How to put the desk together.

Exceptional Care for Your Valued Client

It's easy to write directions for a local person, or put together instructions for someone in the industry, but doing so for a novice or newcomer, which is who you need to write directions and instructions for in the first place, requires attention to detail.

- Take the Main Street exit to First Avenue and turn in at the driveway. Parking is available behind the building.

That may be obvious to locals who know that the business district in your town is on the west side of the freeway, and that First Avenue is actually nowhere near that freeway, however what if your customer is from another state?

- Driving north on the Bob Nicoll Freeway, take the Main Street exit and follow the road left under the freeway. The Remember the Ice corporate office building is 4.2 miles down on your left, after the railroad tracks. For parking, continue down Main Street past our offices one half block to First Avenue. Turn left onto First Avenue, then turn left again into the first driveway and follow the signs to Remember the Ice.

- Driving south on the Bob Nicoll Freeway, take the Main Street exit and merge right onto Main Street. The Remember the Ice corporate office building is 4.2 miles down on your left, after the railroad tracks. For parking, continue down Main Street past our offices one half block to First Avenue. Turn left onto First Avenue, then turn left again into the first driveway and follow the signs to Remember the Ice.

Of course, there has to be a starting point before which you draw the line at responsibility. Getting to the Bob Nicoll Freeway in the first place is going to have to be up to the customer's resourcefulness.

As you sit down and go over the information you provide to valued clients to dissect it for counter-productive words or absence of elegant detail, remember to let this Golden Rule guide you: Deliver information as clearly as you would like it delivered to you. After all, "There is power

Section 2

in the clarity of your articulation." Then kick it up a notch to the Platinum Rule and share the information as they would like to receive it.

The secret to powerful articulation is clarity; clear understanding of what you intend to say, clear understanding of what you mean before you speak, and choosing the right words to make sure your message is clear to those on the receiving end. The most empowering way to deliver that clarity is via Respectful Elegance.

As long as "Respectful" and "Elegance" are guiding your word choice, you will be empowered to communicate effectively. Effective communication delivers positive results; the other party listens, understands, replied positively, received the news well, and/or acted constructively in response. The point of communicating, after all, is to have your needs met. Whether your need is to persuade, educate, clarify, express yourself, receive attention or affection, reach an agreement, or stay in business, communication is what gets you there.

When you pay attention to detail, leave nothing out, use simple and straightforward words without being condescending, make sure your customer understands you, and make sure you make a human connection, you demonstrate Respectful Elegance.

Respectful Elegance requires respect for yourself, respect for your message, respect for your intention, respect for your products and services, respect for your business, and above all: respect for the other person. If you lack respect for your customer, why on earth are you in business?

Exceptional Care for Your Valued Client

Section 2

Chapter 12

Best Practices: Client Service Words and Behavior

LuAnn Buechler has been on the front lines of client service in the very fast-paced, high-pressure world of hospitality for her entire professional life, and her ability to work with the entire spectrum of personalities has become an integral part of her livelihood. She's the one who really got me thinking about the pitfalls behind the phrase *"the customer is always right."* She has seen it in action at its ugliest, and has had to face it down squarely and fairly.

While I object to the words and the message, and work to show you how to choose empowering attitudes to replace it, LuAnn has been challenged countless times to deal successfully with obnoxious customers who wield this attitude like a weapon; I turn to her to talk about how to deal with the angry, unreasonable, unyielding customer with the overblown sense of entitlement.

So the question becomes, *"Bob, LuAnn, how can you use Respectful Elegance to get rid of a customer who is a real jerk?"*

First things first: Pay attention to word choice. Drop the word *"jerk"* because that immediately puts you squarely in the wrong paradigm. A negative word choice attaches and reinforces a negative feeling to the person in front of you. Labeling him a jerk will make it a lot harder to resolve the issue positively, productively and creatively. Name-calling and labeling is disempowering – for both people.

Guard your thoughts. Managing the situation is your responsibility. Begin by mentally referring to him as "customer." When you're grumbling inside your head, say to yourself "this guy is such a customer," and if it's really bad, adjust and begin saying to yourself, "this guy is such a valued *client*" and see how powerful that word choice can be. It's hard to hold on to feelings of resentment when you're simultaneously aware of the fact that he's a valued person.

Exceptional Care for Your Valued Client

LuAnn is so practiced at handling challenging customers she rarely gets her feathers ruffled at all. "When a customer is angry and upset, what you have to remember is what they are really saying is *help me. I can't do this myself; help me.* You're the vehicle for that help, and that's a privilege. Most of the time the solution is easier than what you may have thought,"

I have seen her in action in some pretty tough situations. I have had the privilege of watching her smoothly and confidently handle a client's immediate anxiety in the front of the house, all the while staying on top of chaos behind the scenes. If only that client knew what was happening out of sight; LuAnn gave no indication of anything but smooth waters. Talk about a fantastic example of grace under fire; she really knows how to demonstrate *Respectful Elegance*.

LuAnn has learned the secret to troubleshooting customer angst. Only when you remain calm can you listen to their words and to what's going on behind their words. That is the way to get to the heart of the matter, get the situation resolved, and move on to the next right thing.

Her experience has taught her, "You have to keep in mind that when a customer is in your face, most of the time what they are really doing is asking you to help them. That anger is about need and being afraid their needs will be ignored or trampled on. Sometimes it's about suspicion - it's about suspicion and fear they will be taken advantage of because your knowledge and their ignorance makes them feel vulnerable."

LuAnn cautions us to be aware of the black hole that is customer emotion and distress. Remaining calm and separate in the face of the customer's personal drama or tragic story is as important as remaining calm in the face of anger and panic. It's up to you to be the clear-thinking, clear-speaking and logical one; that's the only way you're going to be able to construct a solid solution. Empathize, show compassion, yet refuse to let your energy, wit and ability get sucked into their emotional maelstrom.

Section 2

Is it heartbreaking to find out that the customer in front of you has flown in for a funeral, broke a heel running to meet her connection in the last airport, found out her luggage never made it, has had no sleep in the past 48 hours and is unable to find her driver's license? Yes. Your heart can and will go out to her. Does that mean you can rent her a car without that license? No. Be kind and compassionate. Help her with public transportation options. If you get too involved with the drama, you will lose time and be far less effective. She needs you to be able to focus.

Practice dealing graciously with needy customers. When the pace picks up and efficiency is the best way to make it through the rush, the last thing you want is a needy customer. There is a difference between a customer who needs information in order to make a decision, and a needy customer who needs to suck up all your attention. A needy customer makes you spell things out with less speed and more detail than the average customer – and repeatedly. She rephrases the same question eight different ways, forcing you to repeat yourself a bunch of times and reassure her that it all makes sense, generally holding her hand until she feels good about the information you gave her.

Face-to-face neediness can drag a simple 10-minute interaction out to an hour; incessant phone calls can stretch a 3-hour job into an hour past closing time You may begin to think that it's almost worth it to send her to your competitor so that she can waste their time. But every customer is precious, and the needy ones can be very loyal.

Respectful Elegance demands that you clearly and politely find a way to tell her you have to break away to get the process started or the work done or the order placed – for her. Respect her enough to be gentle yet firm. Respect the next customer enough to have the courage to close the conversation. Respect yourself enough to have the confidence to know that when you exert control, respectfully, you are indeed showing respect.

Pay attention to why the customer is being needy. Do her questions indicate a lack of faith in her own ability to follow directions? Reassure her that the worst that could happen is manageable and okay. Is she making it painfully obvious that she's finding it next to impossible to let

Exceptional Care for Your Valued Client

go and trust you to do your job? Reassure her you stand behind your work and that if there are any mistakes or problems you will fix them for her – but you have to get started first.

"My crew is going to take care of you. As soon as we isolate the leak in your roof we'll let you know what it's going to cost and how long it will take, and then get to work. But we have to get up there first."

"Yes, but, what if… ?"

"That's all I know right now. I want to give you answers, but being down here instead of up there is stopping me."

"I'm just worried that…"

"I understand. And I have to go up on the roof now. I have another appointment after this one. I will be back within 15 minutes."

When it comes to the angry or aggressive customer, maintaining your composure is yet another form of respectful elegance. It is the only way to handle undignified behavior with dignity.

Examine your motives. If you think the goal is to get rid of the customer, how does that empower either of you? Getting rid of someone is a motive that is beneath respectful elegance. It's time to shift the paradigm. This thought process requires you to check yourself and say, "If I'm unable to employ Respectful Elegance in this act; then I'd better re-evaluate my purpose. So, what does the customer want that I can help with?"

Perhaps the customer wants what he wants NOW, and having to wait is making him very angry. He needs an explanation that makes sense, an apology if appropriate, an assurance no one is taking advantage of him or devaluing his time by working slowly, or whatever else he's worried about.

LuAnn's instructions are to repeat back to the customer a summary of what he is telling you the problem is. Focus on what the customer is saying with this question in mind: "What can I do to fix that?" When

Section 2

you ask yourself this question, you stimulate your thought processes to work in the right direction: Solution.

"What I hear from you is; we got your order wrong." What can I do to fix that? I can make sure the order is resubmitted correctly and offer something in return for the wait. A discount? A gift certificate for the next visit?

"What I hear from you is; the instructions make no sense. Getting from step four to step five is confusing?" What can I do to fix that? I can zero in on the confusion and figure out a way to re-explain what needs to be done so the individual in front of me understands it. I can take a few extra minutes of my time to demonstrate or diagram what I'm talking about.

"What I hear you saying is; you would be more comfortable with landmarks than street signs?" What can I do to fix that? I can think about the directions to my business and the landmarks along the way. I can mentally count how many major intersections there are before she has to turn left at the gas station. I can tell which fast food restaurant to look for and which bank is right before our driveway.

"What I hear you saying is; you are hot and frustrated, and tired of waiting." What can I do to fix that? Nothing. The delay is beyond my control. However, I can sympathize and offer my compassion and whatever tools I have at hand to help with comfort. I can give him water, or direct him to a place that can. I can treat him with respect by demonstrating I expect him to be smart enough to understand the heat and delay are beyond my control; that means leaving whining and impatience out of my voice when I explain that delay, even if it is for the 18th time.

In LuAnn's experience, most of the time the solution is easier than what either of you may have anticipated. It helps when both of you has a clearer understanding of his request or concern.

This is great advice, even when there are no problems in sight. "Okay, what I hear you saying Is; you want a non-smoking room above the

Exceptional Care for Your Valued Client

fourth floor with an ocean room? I want to make sure I know exactly what you're looking for."

Often, what you repeat back to them is different from what they're trying to say. That's great! If you make it clear you are misunderstanding them, they can rephrase what they're saying; at the very least they will realize they're failing to communicate their need.

In extreme situations, when communication has broken down and the pressure is getting to you, excuse yourself. Asking a co-worker to step in can be helpful in a number of ways. A fresh face can help bring down a temper on the rise because your face is being associated with negative feelings. A fresh set of eyes may see a simple solution where neither one of you saw it before. A fresh set of ears may pick up on a detail you missed.

The best person to bring into the situation is one who has more knowledge, information, experience or authority than you. This person will be able to resolve the situation – either by taking over and doing things differently, or by taking over and doing them exactly the way you were doing them.

"Sir, I can see we seem to be making no progress. If you will excuse me for just a moment, I'm going to find another representative who may be able to resolve this issue for you." Recognize when you and your face have become a wall, admit when you and the customer are at an impasse, and do something about it.

And if the buck stops with you? What if you're the manager, top of the exceptional care food chain, or the owner of the business, and the customer has become a bully? It's actually very simple. You have the authority to end the stand-off, so do it. Be clear, succinct, and polite, and guide the customer to the door and away from draining the energy from your business as efficiently as possible. There is a point at which the value of having him leave outweighs the value of having him as a customer.

Section 2

"Sir, I appreciate your situation, unfortunately it is clear that we are unable to help you. I regret that there is nothing further we can do." And then be quiet. That's all you need to say. Sometimes, the most gracious thing you can do for everyone concerned is move him along to the next destination. Employ Respectful Elegance even if you're sure you'll never see him again; the way he thinks and talks about you when he leaves matters.

First you need to practice Respectful Elegance until you own it; then dealing with those who are less than gracious will barely ruffle your feathers – at least on the outside.

When it comes to providing Exceptional Care, Respectful Elegance is about making the extra effort to connect positively with your customer, and as I started to explain before, it's about empowering your customer to rely on you as a resource that can be trusted.

If you're having a challenge delivering on your contract, whether it be prompt service or clear skies, inform your customer. Have an alternative ready to offer.

Let them know if you are swamped and they will have to wait longer than usual to get your undivided attention. That's respect, and it's appreciated.

LuAnn cites a story shared by a friend who needed help figuring out how to solve a problem with a piece of equipment. He put a service call through to the manufacturer's help desk and got a pre-recorded message telling him that there were 12 people ahead of him and an approximation of his wait time. Because he knew what to expect, he was empowered to make the decision to put the call on speakerphone and tinker with the piece of equipment while he waited. He solved the problem before they got to him and hung up, thinking nothing more about it.

This triggered a dropped call report in the company's system, and the next day LuAnn's friend was contacted by a supervisor who was following up to find out if he still needed help. The company expected

Exceptional Care for Your Valued Client

their supervisors to reach out to the customers who were unable to get through quickly to make sure they were taken care of. LuAnn says that act made an impression on her friend – and on her – and the company now has two loyal customers for life.

This story is an example of how providing clear and honest information to your customer is a good thing. If the lines are really long, let them know. If you're struggling with half of your usual staff due to illnesses or holidays, let your customers know. Have a back-up plan.

Allow your customers' presence to be recorded and hold their place for them in a "virtual" line until it's their turn. This is a common practice for busy restaurants and theme parks. Especially at theme parks, families can have their place in line "held" for them while they go off and do other things, knowing that if they return within a certain window of time they have a guaranteed spot up where the line would have moved to if they had been in it.

Be pro-active and call customers with appointments for less-than-urgent issues to offer them alternative dates and times. Make sure you convey the idea you are giving them some kind of advantage that shows your friendly interest in making their lives a little smoother.

If there's a strong chance that the skies are going to open up on an April wedding let the happy couple know, make plans for shelter, and create a message that lets the guests know what to expect in case of rain.

Anticipating what your clients will need to stay in your business bubble is a skill that is directly related to Respectful Elegance.

If you want to be able to trust your employees to deliver on all of the above, think on their feet, and act as you would act in the face of a challenging situation, you have to be very clear about your expectations. Anything less falls short of Respectful Elegance.

LuAnn enjoys telling a story about a recent trip to a steakhouse in Lansing, Michigan. All of the pieces were in place:

Section 2

The style was to have peanut shells strewn over the floor, yet it was done well and the dining room was clean. The hostess was pleasant and seated them promptly. Although it was fairly busy, the server came to the table right away and introduced himself. The food came out hot and fast, to their specifications, and it was very good. The hostess, manager and another server each stopped by the table at some point during the meal to check on them.

"Around us, the staff cleared off tables, refilled condiments and wiped down chairs and tables so that the next group of diners could be seated. They pitched in and help each other, friendly banter and teamwork were obviously the norm," LuAnn remembers. "Regardless of what was going on, each employee looked clean and sharp when customers walked in."

These are all signs of a well-run establishment. However, what impressed LuAnn was something the server told her. He introduced himself as Mitchell on his first visit to the table, and LuAnn, looking for his nametag to help her remember, was compelled to ask why he was without one.

"We are asked to go without name tags," Mitchell replied. "It is our job to make an impression so you remember our name."

And he did. The desire for this group of people to remember his name and ask for him on a return visit motivated him to connect, to be attentive, to remember little things about each of them, like who had asked for extra gravy and who was going through the sweet tea like their mouth was on fire.

Mitchell, knowing that he was expected to behave in a way that would make his guests remember his name, employed Respectful Elegance in all of his encounters with them. He may have been unaware that I use those words to describe his actions, yet that is what he was doing. His boss empowered him to act with dignity and succor.

Another of our friends shares a story about finding a fly in her salad at a restaurant several years ago. This particular woman is easily put off

Exceptional Care for Your Valued Client

by bad service, and will refuse to return to any restaurant within an entire chain if she has a truly bad experience in just one of them.

When she asked her server to get the manager, she was already disgusted. How nasty did a kitchen have to be to have dead flies in the salad? This was going to be a quick conversation and then she would be done with this place forever.

The manager came over to the table and did something totally unexpected. She apologized and then explained that yes, every once in a while a fly will get into the salad. She explained the process for preparing and storing salads in the kitchen, and how very rarely a fly can get in. She did say it was unacceptable that the server had brought it to the table without paying attention to what was on the plate. While she apologized and clearly regretted the incident, she made no pretense that it never happened. The fact that she took the time to listen to my friend, empathize, and then explain intelligently, coupled with her honesty and ability to take responsibility made an impression. Obviously, this manager took the situation seriously. The restaurant paid for the salad, of course, and my friend has actually been back several times.

Knowing her as I do, I was surprised by this story's ending. The manager's actions really underlined what I have been saying about the impact using Respectful Elegance has on your customer's opinion of you, and willingness to accept mistakes, return to do business with you in spite of a mishap, and encourage others to do the same.

Section 2

Section 2 Exercises

Learning How to Speak and Act to Empower Yourself AND Your Client

In the first section of the book we focused on identifying (K)notty Words. For your exercises you were asked to look at your marketing materials, website content, phone scripts, policy manuals, customer service scripts, anything in writing that has to do with how you provide Exceptional Care for Your Valued Client.

The chapters in Section 2 reminded you about the Process of Education and Re-Education; discussed Empowering vs. Disempowering Word Choice; introduced you to the concept of Respectful Elegance; and focused on Best Practices including "What I hear you saying is…"

For your first exercise, identify a behavior in the delivery of your exceptional care you know will and can be enhanced by making a significant change in the way you act toward your customers/clients.

You are raising your awareness about this behavior and are on the path of developing a higher level of *Exceptional Care for Your Valued Client*. Think about a shift that is as major as driving on the other side of the road; just like in a different country from where you learned how to drive.

Write this behavior down. Spend some time thinking about how you (your Company) first learned this behavior. Take an unbiased look at it, checking your ego at the door, and be proactive in identifying the changes you (your employees) would like to make to raise the bar in providing *Exceptional Care for Your Valued Client*.

Because this is a significant shift in behavior it will feel awkward at first. You may want to revert back to an earlier, more comfortable place.

STOP!!!

Exceptional Care for Your Valued Client

Remember that in order to make the shift, you will have to go through Cognitive-Emotive Dissonance. (This is a good thing!) Identify what the C-E D is, and focus on it. Whatever level you are in your company, remember you have ownership. Exceptional Care comes from the individuals that make up a company.

For your second exercise, pay particular attention to your *shoulds* and *absolutes*. Re-frame them in both your written and spoken words with your clients and fellow employees. Identify your most common phrases and brain storm on how to change them.

Gather as a team in the break room and have a discussion about it. Heck, order a couple of Pizzas, a spinach salad, and some water and sodas and have a good time working at it.

Here is your first one:

The Customer is Always Right!!!

Yikes! What a place to start. It *is* the big elephant and it *is* taking up most of the space in the room. You might as well get started on it a bite at a time.

Here are some of the ones from Chapter 8:

- "You always give me the run-around"
- "You guys always make me wait"
- "You're always late with your deliveries"
- "You always screw up my order somehow"
- "It always ends up more expensive than you said it would be"
- "You never return my phone calls"
- "You never show up on time"
- "You never come through on your promises"
- "You never get my order right"
- "I never get a straight answer"

Section 2

For your third exercise, combine what you learned in Chapters 10-11 about *Respectful Elegance* and combine it with LuAnn's mantra from Chapter 12, "What I hear you saying is...", while developing a new philosophy providing *Exceptional Care for Your Valued Client*. Really pay attention to treating your client the way they would like to be treated. Learn more about them. Pay attention to them. They are your reason for being in business.

Your objective is to find and keep your clients and customers. How are you doing so far? If you keep doing what you have consistently done, you will continue to get what you have consistently got.

Make your re-framing change. Shift your paradigm and embrace your empowering alternatives.

"Beginning is half done." ~~ *Dr. Robert Schuller*

Exceptional Care for Your Valued Client

SECTION 3

The Whole Package: Delivery and Results

Chapter 13:   Physiology and Congruency

Chapter 14:   Building a Framework of Rapport

Chapter 15:   Forget Price and Keep Value

Exercises for Section 3

Exceptional Care for Your Valued Client

Section 3

Chapter 13

Physiology and Congruency

Physiology and congruency are key elements in that "complexity in communication" I have alluded to in previous chapters. Without them, you run the very real risk of coming across as either robotic, disconnected, unconcerned, or downright rude. They are important puzzle pieces whose absence can even be detected across phone lines.

Choosing the best words to speak to customers is only the beginning of communicating with them. It's a step up from paying little or no attention to what you're saying, but it's just the first one. The way you speak and how you hold yourself when you speak are every bit as important as good word choice.

To put it simply, physiology can best be described as stance, body language, and tone of voice.

Congruency happens when what you're saying is in synch with your physiology. The old saying, "actions speak louder than words" is absolutely correct. Yes, I chose to say "absolutely;" your actions, your physiology, will scream "liar!" louder than anything coming out of your mouth if you are insincere. Likewise, if you are sincere; your physiology will back your words up like a choir of angels ready to testify to the truth of what you're saying.

The backbone of physiology and congruency is intention. Attempt as you might to quash vocal and physical cues you put out there when you communicate; if you're hiding something you will inevitably give yourself away – and then watch out. Remember what I said earlier about mind-set and how important it is? Your frame of mind, your intention, dictates your physiology.

Body language is loaded with conscious and sub-conscious cues that the other person will read and interpret as quickly and completely as they

Exceptional Care for Your Valued Client

hear and interpret your words – sometimes faster. Verbalize "yes" while you're wagging your head back and forth and see what the other person's face registers. Distrust will show up somewhere.

Picture a man standing in front of you with his arms folded across his chest and a scowl on his face. Is he listening to you? Is he open and receptive to what you're saying? No. He is indicating a stubborn refusal to accept your information, explanation or point of view. What if he smiles? Are you going to trust it? In that situation, a smile from this man would make me very suspicious.

Now picture the same man with his hands held loosely by his sides, eyes looking into yours then moving down to the left every so often as he nods his head slowly up and down. Is he listening? Is he open to what you're saying? Yes. He's agreeable to the possibility. In fact, his eyes sliding down and to the left indicate he's considering it carefully. Smile or no smile, you know he's being open-minded and receptive.

We human beings have been programmed to recognize body language cues. This kind of programming is so deeply ingrained in our psyches that subconsciously at least we rely on them more heavily than we rely on verbal cues.

Perhaps this is why it rankles me when a server at a restaurant places a dish at the table without interest and/or looking at me. Or why I stopped going to my favorite deli because they left a teenager in charge who let three minutes pass before coming out to greet me, and then finished his text before looking up to speak. These actions were clear indications that I was unworthy of either person's concern, regardless of what they had to say about it.

When the server came back to the table and asked if we had everything we needed while her eyes tracked what was going on at her other tables in the restaurant, do you think my wife and I believed she cared? Do you think we left a tip that indicated we believed we were properly taken care of? If we return to that restaurant, will we hope to be seated in her section, or hope to avoid a repeat of our previous experience?

Section 3

When the teen at the deli walked out of the back room with the phone in his hand, and decided against putting it down or away, do you think I believed I was his top priority and that he would make my order the right way, without texting in between tasks? Do you think I decided to stick around to find out?

For some people, Exceptional Care for their valued client is effortless. For the rest of us, it's a learned skill. It can seem daunting to the uninitiated.

"I'm supposed to remember what? Posture, tone of voice, eye contact, what I'm doing with my hands, how to control my face – all at once? I have to pretend to care AND choose the right words? How am I supposed to do that, Bob?!?"

Check your intention. Pretending to care is the wrong goal; figuring out how to care is the key to success. I'll talk more about that in the chapter on the ABCs of Emotion.

If, in the process of delivering food to a table, you feel the need to ward off a sense of being overwhelmed by constantly scanning all the tables in your section to stay on top of them, then that is how your body language will read. You can smile and drop words that say you care about my experience, however the speed of your words, the darting of your eyes, the unconscious turning of your body in the direction you wish you were heading off in already will reveal that your mind is elsewhere.

If you consider it a key part of your role to make sure you're available to refill my ice tea, that it makes you happy when my wife and I have everything we need and have good opinions about the food, and you want to create a signature moment that will bring us back, then you will behave differently at my table. My wife and I will become a destination, rather than another island in the stream. And what do you do at a destination? You stop, stay a minute, check things out, engage. You ask more specific questions. "I see you're on your second refill. Would you like me to bring a pitcher to the table? How do you like those garlic mashed potatoes? Was I right? Told you they are better than the fries."

Exceptional Care for Your Valued Client

Physiology has two roles. On the one hand, it confirms or denies what you're saying as sincere by sending unmistakable signals of your true intentions to the other party. On the other, and equally interesting hand, altering your physiology alters your mind-set and ultimately your word choice.

If you are feeling overwhelmed and anxious about getting to the party at the next table, take physical action. Stop at my table and turn to face me. Rest your hand on the back of a chair. Consciously block out the other tables, just for a minute, and deliberately identify something unique in the situation. "Hmm... this guest has had two refills already. I'll ask about that..."

Stop texting and then put the phone down, preferably in another room, definitely out of reach. Carrying it in your pocket provides too much temptation to pull it out again if it rings or vibrates. Put it down. Physically separate yourself from the object so that you can mentally separate yourself from it and proceed to engage.

The conscious act of putting down the toy, tool, phone or notepad will shift your focus, and your paradigm, from attending to what you were doing to attending to the customer. Likewise, the act of picking up the toy, tool, phone or notepad, if that's what you use when you're paying attention to a customer, will do the same job. Changing your physiology will snap your intention back into place.

Regardless of whether you are working on spreadsheets, placing orders, planning the marketing budget for the next year or writing the checks that keep the lights on, when a customer enters your space, take action. Move yourself in their direction. Look up from the computer, move the papers from the middle of the desk to the side. Stand up. Minimize the budget on your screen. Do whatever it takes to shift your eyes to your customer and away from temptation.

It seems like a lot to remember, yet here's the secret: If it's sincere, there's no thinking, scheming or planning necessary; the congruency happens naturally. It's when you're insincere that you have to worry.

Section 3

There are some pretty important cues I'd like to highlight for you here. These are the cues that set off the chain reaction of other cues that attach and follow. They include, among others, making eye contact, facing the customer squarely, smiling while you speak, lifting your head and straightening your posture.

If you're in the habit of carrying on a conversation or imparting information while you're looking down and/or multi-tasking, stop it. Change now. Start training yourself to look up and quiet your hands the moment you need to greet or speak to a customer/client.

That physical movement will signal to your brain you are about to change your train of thought; you are tuning in to what's in front of you and your focus will follow suit.

Once you have lifted your head, deliberately seek a connection through eye contact. Making eye contact is a sign of a healthy self-image, as well as a sign you are being honest, have nothing to hide, and are fully confident that you can back up what you're saying. "Challenge me if you'd like; I believe in what I'm saying, and I believe I'm capable of delivering on it. I have pride and integrity."

Well guess what? Making eye contact also helps to build a healthy self-image. When you look someone in the eye and they look right back at you, the connection is immediate and complete. "You are worth looking at. You are worth talking to. You are worth listening to. You are worthy of the truth." Even if, realistically, you're just worthy of the 30 seconds it takes to say hello and take your latte order, it's important enough that the absence of eye contact is offensive.

If this is an unfamiliar or uncomfortable act for you, get over it for your own sake. Seriously, get it under your own control. Start practicing now. Lift your chin. Raise your eyes towards that other set across from you. Note how your shoulders pull back a little and your spine is inclined to straighten. It's so much easier to smile when your chin is lifted and your eye-line is higher than the horizon. That's physiology, or physical stance, affecting your mood and body language. The response to this

Exceptional Care for Your Valued Client

action will be positive. A person with straight back, open shoulders, lifted chin and eyes that seek contact has nothing to hide. This stance is trustworthy.

Whether you deal with customers in person or over the phone, altering your physical features to form a smile will improve your attitude, the other person's attitude, and help you exude warmth, friendliness and, here we are again: Trustworthiness.

Your physiology will affect how you interact with the customer, and it will establish how the customer perceives you – on both a conscious and sub-conscious level. Without the congruence of physiology and word choice, you will be unable to build bridges of trust, loyalty and reliability. Remember, congruence is achieved when intention, word choice and physiology all match. All of the other elements can be in place, yet it only takes one missing piece to derail the best plans for Exceptional Care.

Begin with intention and build from there. Sincere intention will guide stance, tone of voice, how fast you talk, and word choice. It will influence and control your body language.

When intention is out of synch with the rest of your message, you will struggle to get out of the starting gate.

Patricia ran a small, upscale boutique in a quaint business district within minutes of several well-to-do suburbs. Her niche was "cool mom" and she made sure her store carried high-end clothing, shoes and accessories that teenage girls and women in their early 20s would be drawn to but unable to afford, thus making it more appealing to the youthful, energetic mom in her 30s and 40s. Apparently, a little envy from the daughter can be a good thing for the mother.

She very deliberately created an atmosphere in her boutique declaring; young and hip is a state of mind, taste and sophistication come with experience, and that the mothers of teenagers still have it going on, are old enough to afford it and self-confident enough to carry it off.

Section 3

Patricia made sure the music playing was a blend of pop and independent female artists in their 30s and 40s, some in other languages and all at background level. She deliberately stocked the counter area with CDs featuring the music she played to reinforce the subliminal connection.

Understanding the contradiction between the maturing tastes of her clients and their need to express their inner youthfulness, she chose wall colors and décor that spoke of elegance, warmth and a welcoming atmosphere, with splashes of color and bold statements where she wanted to draw attention. She paid attention to detail with an eye to upscale tastes; heavily framed mirrors and solid, upholstered furniture in the well-lit dressing rooms, stylish lighting fixtures and hardware, wooden coat hangers, and hand-written price tags. The clothing and accessories themselves spoke fun and young; styles, colors and cuts mimicked those in stores for younger women but were of higher quality and designed to fit a woman's shape better than a girl's.

If she had been targeting teenagers and 20-somethings, Patricia would have chosen pop, hip-hop and other top-40 "bubblegum" music to be played loud enough to be in the foreground of hearing. She would have raised the energy level further with brightly painted walls, highly reflective surfaces and decorations that screamed "look how cool I am!" It would have been a store appropriate to loud chatter, giggling, and girlfriends trying things on in packs without the need or desire for some salesperson to bother them. The onus would be on trend rather than style, with quickly rotating stock and clearance bins.

Patricia prided herself on paying attention to what her clientele would feel comfortable with and respond to. When she personally spent time working in her boutique she wore designer jeans, heels made for the dance floor, trendy tops and overstated accessories right from the display cabinets. She insisted that her employees, all chosen for their youth and taste in clothing, also pay close attention to what they wore. They had to look like they knew all about fashion at all times; nothing unprofessional, food court, or skate-park; everything fun, flirty and sophisticated.

Exceptional Care for Your Valued Client

All the pieces were in place, and yet something was off. Something was missing, and Patricia was unable to put her finger on it. Cool moms would walk into the store, obviously fall in love with the setting, the clothing, the purses and the jewelry, but for all their obvious delight, sales were pretty low, up-sells were virtually non-existent, and she rarely saw the same woman come in and make a purchase more than once or twice.

None of her employees was rude. Each went about her business, performing tasks dutifully and efficiently, greeting customers pleasantly, and being nice and respectful young women. No one was obtrusive, inappropriate, unprofessional or immature. Cell-phones had been banned from the floor, trash was whisked away before it hit the ground, and the displays were kept clean, tidy and appealing. And yet, something was definitely missing from the store.

Something was missing on a personal level for Patricia, too. An outgoing, social person, she had chosen to build a business around playful fashion just for energetic, stylish women in her age group for the very reason that it would attract her favorite kind of people to her life.

She envisioned a full, fun place where friends could hang out and shop, and where she, as the fun and friendly owner, could get to know her customers and cultivate friendships with them. She had plans to host after-hour networking parties and invitation-only sneak peek evenings for her best customers when new inventory hit the store; she wanted to be a feature in these fabulous women's lives.

Patricia chose to open her boutique because she loved people. She imagined spending her time helping customers find the perfect little something to boost their spirits, the perfect dress to remind a tired mom that the bombshell inside was allowed to come out and play, the perfect bangles and earrings to set off a new haircut and embolden a new attitude. Patricia knew women in their 30s and 40s, the facets of their lives that kept them busy, the small gestures and little treasures that could put a bounce in their step.

Section 3

She deliberately and thoughtfully invested in filling her space with warmth, light and youthful energy to draw them to her so she could give back the love and friendship so many women had given to her over the years.

Instead, the boutique felt stale. With each passing day, Patricia felt more isolated, less empowered to have any kind of impact on anyone's life, and more like a failure who was in over her head. She was beginning to think that her sense of style was so wrong that it repelled people from her door. What if the truth of the matter was that her taste was so off the mark and her assessment of the market was so backwards that her boutique was a joke? What if the reason so few customers ever came back was because she really had terrible taste and knew nothing about fashion, let alone style? Her self-esteem was definitely taking a hit.

One Sunday afternoon, Patricia found herself in line at a big box store with a cart full of random gardening tools, young plants and bulbs for her home. Her mind was anywhere but on her business; she was hoping that a day of digging in the earth would distract her from what was beginning to feel like failure at the boutique.

And so she was a million miles away when the line moved forward. She roused herself and wheeled her cart up to the cash register, ready to respond nicely to the cashier's greeting. However, instead of a friendly, upbeat hello, Patricia was greeted by an expressionless face and something unintelligible grunted at her from across the counter. "*I know how she feels*," Patricia sighed to herself, feeling even lower than before.

The cashier scanned each of the items, bagged them, and waited patiently for Patricia to slide her card through the machine and punch in the numbers to complete the transaction. On a whim and with a sense of solidarity for the cashier because bad days can be hard to shake, Patricia smiled at the young woman and said, "I hope your day gets better soon."

To which the young woman replied, "Oh my day's fine. I just don't do the whole "smiling" thing. I don't like to talk to people all that much."

Exceptional Care for Your Valued Client

Patricia wheeled her cart away, stunned. Her mind was reeling. Would she ever employ a person who refused to smile and engage in conversation, let alone place them in a customer service position? Was there more to it? She started to take it personally. Was it her race, her age, the way she dressed or her hair style? She walked away with an uneasy feeling that somehow she was inadequate and out of place.

She unloaded the cart and sat in her car for a good long time, thinking over the strange encounter. There was something about it that was familiar. Somewhere in the back of her mind an idea was dawning. By the time she got home, she had formed a plan, and with renewed energy decided to test her theory out the very next day.

Patricia spent the morning in the store, keeping her hands busy and her eyes on her employees as they greeted each customer. To a person, they were polite, doing exactly as Patricia had instructed them. However, they delivered their greetings on the move, as they bustled about completing other tasks, and kept moving in a bee-line past the customer when they'd check in to see if anything was needed. The customer was being treated like a passerby rather than a destination.

Patricia had noticed this behavior in other stores, especially the stores where her teenagers shopped, and especially during the holidays or when it was busy. It was as if the salesperson was on a merry-go-round, saying, "Here I am, here to help you, checking in as I go by, nothing you need? Okay, bye-bye till the next go 'round, oh look my hands are full, I'm very important, here I am, here to help you, checking in as I go by..." This kind of customer service irked her, but her kids thought she was weird for noticing.

The more Patricia watched her own employees, the more she realized that her recent epiphany was spot on: The missing piece to the puzzle was in the way the young sales staff interacted with the customers. It was clear that the teenagers and 20-somethings, though polite and knowledgeable, had little or no idea how to relate to the older women who entered the shop, and vice versa.

Section 3

It became painfully obvious when a customer of about 35 stepped out of a dressing room in a stunning outfit, only to become paralyzed in front of the mirror. Patricia glanced around to see who was on the floor; someone needed to approach the woman and help her out.

Patricia caught the eye of Karen, the closest employee, and tipped her head in the customer's direction. Karen happily obliged, and Patricia moved in closer to hear what they were saying.

"Those two pieces work really well together," Karen said on her approach, "the blue is perfect on you."

"Thank you, but I'm worried about this skirt," the woman said, twisting in front of the 3-way mirror to try to see it better from different angles.

"It fits beautifully," Karen confirmed. "Is it comfortable? Can I get you another size? We also have it in khaki."

"Oh yes, it's fine. I'm worried about the length."

"You definitely have the legs to pull it off. Pilates?"

Karen was trying, but missing the point. Patricia noted the little crease of frustration on the woman's brow and the slightly puckered lips and joined the group to help out.

"I see what you mean," Patricia said to the woman's reflection, making it obvious that she was looking at the hem of the skirt and taking her concern seriously. "It's a little on the short side for a family brunch. This would definitely go better with wine tasting or maybe date night with your husband on one of these warm summer nights. It needs really cute flats or sandals; heels would be tacky. We have the cutest Roman sandals that just came in. Karen, can you grab a pair in gold for her?"

The woman showed relief, agreed that the sandals made the outfit but a white top would work better, and left happy. In the meantime, Patricia enjoyed making small talk with her customer, suggesting a winery to

Exceptional Care for Your Valued Client

visit and reiterating the fact that the skirt would be most flattering with flat shoes instead of high heels. What remained unspoken was the question: "Am I too old for this?" and the honest answer, which would have been: "You are if you try to wear heels with it; you will look like you're trying too hard to compete with your daughter."

This exchange was further proof to Patricia that she had made a fundamental mistake in one of the key components of her business. The people entrusted to do the actual communicating were unable to connect with the customers. Their efforts, as well-meaning as they were, failed to ring true and often made customers uncomfortable.

Had she really expected someone like Karen, who was about 10 years away from wondering if a skirt was age-appropriate on her, to be able to find the language and sincerity to address that very concern with a woman approaching 40?

Later in the day, Patricia observed another of her salespeople, Hannah, awkwardly making small talk with a different customer as she was ringing up her sale. It was painful to watch. Intelligent, articulate Hannah was standing there letting her voice trail off at the end of each sentence, inserting "like" after every other word, and being over-zealous in her responses. The customer stood there, patiently letting the effusive "awesomes" and "totally cutes" slide past her as she waited for her bag, but it was obvious that Hannah was failing to make a good impression.

"Okay, Hannah. What on earth was that?" Patricia asked as soon as the customer had left.

"Ugh. I felt like such an idiot. She totally reminded me of one of my mom's friends," she screwed up her nose, "I never know what to say to them. They're so, you know."

"I think I do," Patricia said. "They're so different from you?"

"They're trying too hard. It's totally embarrassing."

Section 3

Uh-oh. Warning bells went off in Patricia's head. When it came to selling the "cool mom" image, Hannah was severely handicapped; she lacked respect or appreciation for its value. Clearly, Hannah had been thinking and acting in terms of "us" and "them," and the age difference indicated a cultural divide she had no clue how to cross.

Patricia realized that for the sake of her business, she was going to have to either train Hannah to think and feel differently about their target demographic, or remove her from the job.

Everything else was in place; the music, the lighting, the clothing, the mannequins and furnishings. It was time to pull the salespeople into congruence with the environment. She started implementing training sessions designed to teach her staff specific skills like how to decipher what a 35-year-old woman is asking when she says she's worried about a short skirt.

"Hannah, I want you to shadow Julia for a while," Patricia decided. "Pay attention to how she acts around women like that, the ones who remind you of your mom and her friends. They trust Julia even though she's a lot younger. I think it's because Julia is obviously comfortable with them and can find things to talk about that have nothing to do with age."

"My mom and I have nothing in common," Hannah said. "And her friends think they're so hot, but they're just annoying."

Julia said, "My mom and I hang out all the time, and her friends are a lot of fun. There's always something to talk about. You can totally eavesdrop when I'm talking to a customer. Join in if you want. You'll see. Some pretty cool people come in here; it's fun."

Patricia kept an eye on Hannah and Julia, and after a shaky start, Hannah started to relax and enjoy the customers, and the sneering attitude shifted into one of respect, then appreciation.

As she continued to observe her employees and empower them to slow down and approach each customer as a destination rather than a blip

Exceptional Care for Your Valued Client

on the radar, and to recognize and address the most common concerns of the women who came into the boutique, Patricia was rewarded by obvious returns on her investment of time and attention.

Sales, especially up-sells, strengthened and stabilized; the frequency of return shoppers sky-rocketed; and the store filled up with friendly chatter as it became known as a fun place to shop or just stop by and say hi. She began to host after-hours get-togethers, events and networking mixers in the shop, and saw her business grow into exactly what she had imagined and worked for all along.

Patricia had set out with the greatest of intentions, and took great care to make sure every aspect of her business reflected them. As soon as she identified the missing component, which was a sales staff that shared her understanding of their average customer, she was able to provide a solution through a process of education and re-education for each sales person. She trained them to pay attention to physiology and congruency, and reaped the rewards.

Communication requires more than opening your mouth to speak. Communication is a complex arrangement of components, all swinging out from and anchored to the heart of the matter: Intention. When you come from a place of sincerity and *Respectful Elegance*, you can build just about any relationship you choose, with your customers.

When the economy is particularly challenging, or when competitors seem to be cropping up out of nowhere with slashed prices and fancy new marketing campaigns, you must pay extra attention to how every person in your business or organization expresses themselves, verbally and non-verbally.

Let's get down to the nitty-gritty of it. How do you turn communication style into solid, hands-on, real-world results? In the next chapter I focus on just that. I call it the framework of rapport, and it's essential for establishing **Exceptional Care for Your Valued Client** the first time and every time you meet.

Section 3

Chapter 14

Building a Framework of Rapport

In the next couple of chapters I'm going to focus on what I call the Framework of Rapport. I'm going to tell you what it is, show you how to identify when it's in place, and then teach you how to create it with each customer who comes through your door.

Being able to create a Framework of Rapport is critical to being able to provide exceptional care for your valued client.

A Framework of Rapport is a safe place, a comfort zone if you will, where you and your customer can speak clearly, openly and freely. It is more than a place wherein you exchange niceties; it is a place where you put paying attention to your customer into action and watch it pay off. It is up to you to create this framework and lead your customer into it. Within this framework, you can ask for anything and achieve great things.

Have you ever walked into a meeting with a new client, met a neighbor for the first time, or bumped into an old friend you last saw 20 years ago and found you were unexpectedly and delightedly "clicking" with that person? Your energy level is the same; you're both being friendly, open and responsive; your body language and tone of voice are congruent with theirs; and you find you're identifying with each others' point of view with humor and genuine pleasure?

As if by magic, you suddenly have a bond with this virtual stranger. Time flies by and you find you're talking enthusiastically about ideas and events that have little or nothing to do with the reason you met in the first place, yet they somehow reinforce your good feelings and desire to trust this person.

Inevitably, when you finally pull yourself away from a conversation like this, you find that the outcome is that you have agreed on some kind of

Exceptional Care for Your Valued Client

a plan – and whether business or pleasure, the plan involves coming into contact with this person again.

What just happened? Well, a number of things, actually. It started with two people who "tuned in" to each other, and became two people who were "in tune" with each other.

You liked that person, and they liked you. Something about them put you at ease, made you smile, made you feel good about yourself, and made you feel witty and clever and insightful. In return, because you responded to him or her in these positive, empowering ways, you made that person feel all of the above as well. What happens when two people "click" is that they keep bouncing good energy off each other, like a mirror reflecting a mirror reflecting a mirror through infinite reflections. Being in synch with another person is a truly powerful experience.

You can do this with your customers. Regardless of how brief or limited your contact with them, you can create a Framework of Rapport with each one. A smile and eye contact is the beginning of a basic framework of rapport. Infusing humor, lightheartedness, a spirit of cooperation, and even joy is easy to do. How? Simply employ some of that physiology I mentioned before: Smile when you speak.

Repeat the "I'm so happy to see you" cues every time a customer comes in for a soda, and soon making friendly comments based on your observations will flow easily and you will find yourself expanding your relationship. With that, you strengthen the framework. Why make the effort to provide Exceptional Care for your valued client if he's just buying soda? Because you never know (and I do mean never) where a relationship is going to lead.

What if this customer owns the small business next door and wants to find an affordable way to support the community while getting his name out there in the public eye? If you talk to each other it may become sodas one day, co-sponsoring the same local baseball team the next.

What if this customer is a local musician looking for a downtown venue

Section 3

for her jazz band to perform once in a while? Sodas one day, hosting live music that brings 30 extra people in on a Thursday night the next. What if this customer suddenly has a series of training classes and marketing events to organize for her company? Sodas one day, signing a catering contract with a large corporation the next.

When you feel safe in your self-confidence, you feel safe enough take risks. When you feel safe enough to take risks, the doors fly open and in rush opportunity and possibility, excitement and pleasure. I'm talking about big risks and little risks alike. To some people, remarking on a customer's haircut or the fact it has been a while since they've seen her can feel like a huge risk.

Being observant and asking your customers about themselves, where they work, or if they have exciting plans for the weekend – and remembering the details – are the little signs of interest that in turn spark their interest in you. When you start noticing them, they start noticing you.

It goes back to intention. When you walk into a situation with good intentions, you're bringing along expectations of good results. When you show that you care and intend to continue caring about your customer, expect fantastic results. As human beings, we know when we're cared about. This is an extremely powerful energy. Conversely, we know when that care is being faked or forced. You must examine your intention. Why are you there? Why has this customer ventured into your realm? Why is it a good thing to have them there, seeking your services?

Remember how I explained that physiology and word choice have to be congruent or the person you're talking to will be suspicious of you? If you say one thing and your body language means another, few will trust you. They may never know why, but they'll know *"never"* to trust.

That is disappointing, and hard to shake. Establishing trust takes one kind of effort; re-establishing trust after you've broken it, even in the tiniest of ways, takes a much greater effort. Being incongruent can ruin

Exceptional Care for Your Valued Client

a relationship before it has a chance to become one. That's negative power; it's disempowering.

As ruinous as missing the connection between word choice and physiology can be, the opposite is also true. Making that connection creates a Framework of Rapport wherein just about anything can happen. When you do make the connection, you really hit it out of the park – and you can feel it. That's really what this chapter is about.

I live to shift negative paradigms. I get a kick out of performing the old "turn that frown upside-down" trick on people who are having a bad day. When a new client or customer approaches me with frustration, irritation, suspicion or any other kind of negative energy, I make it a point to use the tools I teach to turn the situation around.

Human beings, individuals, can "click" anywhere. You can be hiking in Yosemite National Park and run into another group of hikers and click with equally awestruck individuals. You can be hauling a week's worth of dirty clothes to the Laundromat on a Sunday afternoon and click with someone else who's in the mood to laugh about washing machine mishaps. You can click with the people seated all around you at a baseball stadium, sharing stories and excitement for the team you support, and you can click with just about every person who wants to be your customer. It's completely up to you.

When it comes to Exceptional Care, it's your job to create a successful paradigm with each and every individual who approaches your business. Clicking with a customer creates a fertile ground for an array of opportunities.

Clicking is great; however, you have to remain professional.

You want to take and keep control of every face-to-face and every phone call. You know that you set the tone with word choice and physical demeanor. Now keep it up. Do it with confidence, and do it by paying attention to your customer's needs. If your intention is to meet those needs politely, completely and competently, you're set. They

Section 3

have come to you because you're the person with the knowledge and skills they need; taking control of the conversation is to your customer's benefit.

It's time to understand that this skill is critical to your success. There is a difference between making sure your customer explains what they need and letting them control how and when they get it. If the customer was always right and always knew what he was talking about, he would never need you.

"I know what's wrong with me. I have a cough. I had the same cough four years ago when I was living overseas. I need the doctor to write me a prescription but it's hard for me to get down there to see him." A cough is a symptom of more than one problem. Is it even possible, let alone responsible, for a doctor to prescribe medicine to someone sight-unseen, especially based on a past condition in another country?

"My brother-in-law said I need spark plugs. He knows something about cars. I need to pick my daughter up from school in an hour, so please hurry." If you ran a repair shop would you start working on a car without first discovering for yourself what was really wrong with it? Would you accept the word of some random brother-in-law as valid, or would you get your own technician to diagnose the problem first? Would you start working on the car before or after telling the customer that changing out spark plugs on her particular car is a 3-hour job?

"We're getting married in Anchorage. I hear it rains there in August, but I really want an outdoor wedding and the last thing I want to do is pay for a tent just in case of a few sprinkles." Summer rain in Alaska tends to be torrential. Are you sure you want the customer in charge of this decision? Is it in her best interest to go ahead and plan for a full day of sun and clear skies?

Customers reveal their ignorance with surprising consistency. Being ignorant is different from being unintelligent; ignorance comes from a lack of information while intelligence is the ability to think and process information. Your customer can be ignorant and intelligent at the same

Exceptional Care for Your Valued Client

time. Respectful Elegance demands that you begin building a framework of rapport with him or her based on the assumption that this is the case.

What are some of the most common statements that your customers – potential and existing – make when they call or walk in that make you want to laugh or cry or bang your head against a wall, or all three at once? How do you address them?

In the case of the customer with the cough, it's clear that he wants the cough to go away with as little fuss as possible. He is going to have to make the journey to the doctor's office, so your job is to make it clear you are taking his concerns about that into account as you schedule his appointment. Focus on building a vision in his mind of your office as one of comfort, with friendly, helpful people to attend to his needs. If there's a bus stop or coffee shop right outside your door, say so. If possible, make that journey he dreads seem like an okay way to spend the morning. When it's time to hang up the phone, tell him you're looking forward to seeing him and helping him get into see the doctor to get that cough taken care of as soon as possible. Be a friendly destination.

Removing the option of getting a prescription without a consultation is your responsibility; you have to take control of the situation to get that person in to see the doctor. You can hit him over the head with a flat-out refusal, or make him feel like an idiot with an "I'm talking to an idiot" tone of voice, or you can treat him with respect and invite him to buy into believing your scenario will be of great benefit to him. They all take about the same amount of time, but only the third option creates a framework of rapport. Which one do you think will garner loyalty, erase fear and suspicion, and encourage him to refer his friends and family members? A little extra time and consideration goes a very long way to creating connections and building successful and profitable frameworks of rapport.

When it comes to car repair, there are basically three types of people who show up at a shop: Those who know what's going on under the hood, those who think they know what's going on under the hood, and those who know nothing about what's going on under the hood. Those who know what's going on under the hood have a very clear

Section 3

understanding of the tools, time, and training it takes to do the job right. Those who think they know what's going on under the hood tend to reveal their ignorance or at least the limits of their knowledge very quickly. However, those who think they know what's going on often make a lot of sense to those who know they know nothing because even though their knowledge and experience is limited, it's more than those who know nothing have. The customer with no working knowledge of car repairs is generally anxious that they have some kind of information to give you when they call so that you'll know where to start, and how to proceed.

It's your job to tell them how the process works. Cars come in to your shop every day, and you have a system for dealing with them. You already know where to start, and that's by finding out the cause of the problem before beginning any repairs or replacing any parts. Before you roll up your sleeves and head over to the car, you spend time listening to the customer tell you how the car is behaving, sounding, or even smelling and why it prompted her to bring it to you in the first place.

To shift the customer from her attachment to spark plugs to the possibility that it could be something else (and either way you will have to diagnose it first), you have to create a Framework of Rapport that puts her at ease. You have to instill confidence. With your words and body language; demonstrate you take her seriously. Her concern is now your concern; your priority is to make sure the car runs efficiently, is safe, reliable, and now the car is in your hands, you will do everything in your power to make sure that's exactly what you deliver. And this is when you explain the time it takes to do so.

If you were listening, you also heard that she needs to attend to her responsibilities, like picking up her daughter, and that issue must be addressed. Attending to this concern will plant you squarely in the center of a Framework of Rapport. It's the humanizing part of the business transaction.

Would she like to make an appointment for the following morning? Is she able to leave the car and arrange for someone to pick her and/or

Exceptional Care for Your Valued Client

her daughter up? Would she like to leave the car and take advantage of a loaner car or a discounted rental car – whichever you have to offer? Presenting the options clearly leaves no room for miscommunication: Diagnosing and then addressing the car's problem will take more time than she assumed.

Offered in a friendly, helpful way, these options send another clear message. You care. You listen. You take her concerns and her lifestyle into consideration. Making sure you take the time to do the job right is a priority. Initially, she may have been frustrated to find out her expectations were out of whack, however if you correct her expectations with an attitude of friendly helpfulness you will find she will return to lean on you instead of family members as the source for car knowledge.

Weddings are fantasy events that have to be skillfully translated into reality by someone with both feet planted firmly on the ground. That is why brides and grooms consult professional wedding planners. Weddings are notorious for being fraught with emotion, and re-interpreting the fantasy so that it works in reality can lead to intense disappointment and less than gracious behavior on the part of the person – usually the bride – who is bent on making this momentous occasion happen exactly the way she imagines it.

It takes enormous skill to be able to respect the emotions involved while remaining emotionally detached yet solicitous and completely "available" all at the same time. Your mission is to bring the bride's fantasy to life, andyour job is to tailor that fantasy to fit within reality's limitations. Your client has been told her entire life that her wedding day is her day, that every detail "should" be exactly the way she wants it, and that it's your job to make it happen her way.

That is only partially true; it is your responsibility to identify the pitfalls in the plan and steer her away from errors in judgment that could have disastrous results. The reality of the situation is that while an outdoor summer wedding in Alaska has the potential to be extraordinarily beautiful, it also has the potential to be soaking wet.

Section 3

If the weather co-operates, temperatures will be mild and warm, with light breezes. With vistas that include mountains and ocean, and a landscape lush with the abundance of wildflowers and vegetation larger than life because of the long summer, it's hard to imagine a more idyllic setting for a wedding. However, the warmth brings rain.

When it rains in Anchorage, it pours. It is full and heavy, and drenching. Showers may be relatively short, but they leave their mark. It is your job to spell this out to your client. You must emphasize how ruinous the rain can be if the wedding party were to be caught without shelter. Explain reality in a way that respects and informs her intelligence, painting a picture of what could happen, and then painting her a picture of how her vision can easily encompass the right kind of shelter. You can turn this let-down into another opportunity for her to fantasize about how her dreams could play out in a new setting. Spark her imagination; show her you're excited by the possibilities and she will be, too.

Within the Framework of Rapport you establish with a bride, trust is the most valuable. She must trust you to take her needs and desires seriously, and you must also teach her to trust you to know what you're talking about.

The Framework of Rapport is the only place safe and secure enough for guiding your client to a shift in paradigm. Only within that established relationship can you explore the possibilities and resolve the situation to your client's satisfaction. When one plan fails, the next plan can be awesome – if you have the framework in place.

It is entirely up to you to set the stage and establish the Framework of Rapport. You must take a leadership role right from the start. If your customer has to work at making a pleasant experience out of doing business with you, then you are way off base and way out of line. What you create within each Framework of Rapport is up to you.

Respectful Elegance creates a sense of dignity, mutual respect, warmth, friendliness, care. Make it empowering – for both of you. When you have this Framework of Rapport, you can anticipate good things. Create your framework with an eye to the anticipation of good things, and let

Exceptional Care for Your Valued Client

that attitude lead you to success. If anticipation of good things is the intention that guides your thought, word choice and physiology, then the congruence of these things will bring the good to fruition. It's a very powerful force. It's like keeping your eyes on the prize, the horizon, the road; wherever you keep your eyes, there you go, there you end up.

Section 3

Chapter 15

Forget the Price, Keep the Value

To raise your ability to communicate with clients into the realm of something truly powerful, I want you to broaden your concept of what components go into that communication package. That's why in this chapter I'm going to spend more time discussing the importance of using your physical space as a powerful tool in your framework building kit. When you have a business that depends on customers coming to you, returning to you, and bringing their friends to you, it really is in your best interest to expand the framework of rapport to your entire space.

You set the tone with every detail you connect to your business. Look around your shop, restaurant, office; take note of the physical space. Is it clean? How old is the paint? What else is on the wall, and does it look nice or does it look like you slapped it up there without much thought? Are the windows clean? What about the floor? As with Patricia's boutique, do the fittings and merchandizing tools match what you're selling? Patricia went to a lot of trouble to make sure the look and feel of her store lent itself to the prices she set for the actual merchandise. She paid attention to the details that supported the value of a shopping experience in her boutique as well as the value of the high-quality products she carries.

Patricia set her store up to facilitate "clicking" with the women who make up her most desired clients. By training her salespeople to find better ways to connect with these women, she taught them how to create a framework of rapport. Standing in her store is a desirable experience. Talking with her salespeople is a desirable experience. Therefore, walking around with a shopping bag from Patricia's store is also a desirable experience. Patricia's customers are eager to advertise that they shop there.

Anticipate, expect and intend that every customer is a valued client; treat them with respect, and decline to compromise on the value of what you offer for the sake of one or two "price shoppers." A price shopper is a

Exceptional Care for Your Valued Client

person who is only concerned with finding the best price for a product or service. To a price shopper, everything can be reduced to a commodity, and every commodity is attached to a price tag. In a price shopper's mind, there are no other factors to consider.

The lesson of using physical environment to set the stage for building a framework of rapport revolves around understanding the difference between bargain shoppers and value shoppers, and in recognizing the benefits of letting go of one in order to focus on wooing the other.

You may choose to house your business in a stripped-down, draughty warehouse furniture mart with the faint odor of mold and mildew coming from the back room and "click" with a customer. What kind of customer do you believe would overlook these conditions for the sake of low prices? The kind of customer who will spend an hour getting excited with you about all the different sofas and armchairs on your floor, and how great the prices are, and then walk down the street to the next guy and buy from him because there's no delivery charge, or the same chair is five dollars cheaper. The customer who is all about the price tag has no concept of the value of your time, your expenses, or your experience. He wasted an hour of your time, still left the store looking for a better price, went with your competitor anyway, and probably forgot the name of your business the next day.

I guarantee that customer clicked with you because his standards are as low as yours, and the bargain-basement prices are what brought him to you in the first place. You were both blinded by greed: Yours to make a sale and his to save a buck. This business model works for some people, but chances are if you're reading this book it's because you recognize the value in providing distinctive, quality Exceptional Care.

There's no point in creating an environment that customers will want to return to if neither you nor your customer base has any interest in getting "attached" or establishing a relationship. If you do want your customers, their friends and their family members to keep shopping with you well into the future, you will create the environment that sends those signals loud and clear.

Section 3

I'm sure you are aware of the furniture galleries and the mom-and-pop furniture stores that have been around for decades and quietly boast of customers who bought their first bedroom suite at their store when they were newly-weds, came back for cribs and changing tables, then toddler beds, followed by bunk beds, daybeds, princess canopies and extra-long twins for the teenage athlete, and are now bringing their children in to pick out cribs and changing tables for their new families. Fostering generations of loyalty is a wonderful achievement, and more common than you may think.

It begins and ends with providing exceptional care for your valued client. Value is the word to think about here. You value your client, and your client values you. Ultimately, when our intention is to provide something exceptional, what you're doing is selling value.

Value is a general term with a lot of specifics that define it:

- A comprehensive warranty on your work
- Technicians who have been trained and certified by reputable, recognized institutions
- Associates who have invested in years of higher education to become experts in their field
- A hard-earned, well-established reputation for good work, thorough work, honesty and integrity
- A hard-earned, well-established reputation for using only the best products in the manufacture and/or repair of your products
- Hard-earned, well-established and appropriate reviews on consumer web-sites
- A strong resume of satisfied clients who are chomping at the bit to sing your praises and serve as the best kind of references
- A policy of investing time in explaining details and educating your clients
- The proven ability to come in on time and under budget

Exceptional Care for Your Valued Client

Extra services like free coffee, Wi-Fi and children's play area in the waiting room. (My friend's dentist has flat-screen TV monitors mounted on each chair, noise-canceling headphones and a selection of DVDs so that patients can pretend they're anywhere but getting a root canal).

Clean floors and furniture, updated magazines, colors and décor that match the energy level, the right kind of music – they all lend an atmosphere of competency that are more often noticed by their absence than by their presence, yet have a psychological effect all the same.

When a customer enters your establishment, the physical space makes the first impression. That physical space is filled with sights, sounds, smells and energy. Smiling, cheerful salespeople moving around in a tense room jar with the background. Slow moving, slow talking individuals will hardly instill a sense of confidence in their ability to get work done quickly, shipped off immediately, or rushed through the process to meet a deadline.

Consider walking into a restaurant in an unfamiliar city. You're with your children, ages five and seven. When you walk in, you are struck by all the different signs and photos and knick-knacks on display. The place is bustling and brightly lit, there's some fun music from the 1950s and 60s playing, most of the tables are booths, and three different servers smile and say hello as the hostess, who is decked out in khakis, a polo shirt and sneakers, walks you to your seat, kids menus and crayons in hand.

You know without looking that the kids are going to be happy with their food choices; even the picky 5-year-old will find something she likes. You also know you can relax your parenting style just a little bit; it's going to be okay for the kids to sit on their knees while they color, and it's also going to be okay if they get a little loud.

Within this framework of rapport, the restaurant management can ask you to accept other noises as part of the event, especially the noises of other children. They can ask you to be happy with food served in plastic baskets and wiped up with paper napkins. This is a family restaurant,

Section 3

and you'll get your food quickly, then your check, and be back out in the parking lot before bed time.

What happens when you walk in to a different kind of restaurant, one with subdued lights, unobtrusive and sophisticated jazz wafting in the background, and a hostess wearing a silk blouse, pearl necklace and high heels? As she seats you at a table with a linen tablecloth and upholstered chairs, what kind of parenting mode are you in?

Which of these greetings do you expect from a server in this restaurant?

- Hey y'all, my name's Wendy. Can I get you something to drink?"
- "Good evening, sir. My name is Wendy. I will be your server this evening. Can I interest you and your guests in a beverage before dinner?"

In this restaurant the fresh-cut flowers and candles on each table, silverware, stemware, cloth napkins, and reserved mannerisms of the staff contribute to a framework of rapport wherein the management can ask you, the customer, to make sure your children behave with decorum. They can ask you to wait a little longer between ordering your meal and having it delivered, take a little more time savoring the chef's preparation, and spend a little more money – sometimes a lot more money – for the privilege.

Spending more money on an evening of dining at a fine restaurant is considered "worth it" because of the value that comes along with satiating your appetite this way. Whether you're ordering a hot dog from a street vendor, potato skins from a bartender, chicken fettuccine from a server in a tee-shirt or chicken tetrazzini from a server in a tie, it's ultimately the same thing: You're putting something in your mouth so that you can chew, swallow and digest it. What sends you to the street vendor, bartender, sidewalk cafe or upscale restaurant is an understanding of what you're really paying for before you get there.

If you have $5 in your pocket and a yen to sit in the park on a summer day, what drives you to one hot dog vendor instead of another?

Exceptional Care for Your Valued Client

Chances are, the one you choose is operated by someone who has established a framework of rapport with you. He remembers your name or your "usual" order, knows whether you like ketchup or horseradish, and is fast with his hands so that you can get to that spot in the shade with plenty of lunch hour left to enjoy it.

If, however, you have three clients visiting from Japan and want to make sure they get to experience the best of your city before they leave, chances are that at one point you will want to wine and dine them in a restaurant that embodies elegance, good taste, and a wonderful culinary experience you can brag about and they will remember and be impressed by. That kind of meal is an investment. As a value shopper, you're going to buy in to all that invisible value.

At such a restaurant, a Framework of Rapport has been established wherein the customer asks for a world-class experience and the management asks for a certain level of behavior, a certain level of taste and appreciation, and a certain price point above the average family restaurant.

How you greet and speak to your customer reinforces the framework of rapport that has been established by the physical setting. You have control, even if they begin in a bad mood. You have the communication skills and the ability to choose the most powerful words and phrases, therefore you dictate how the conversation is going to develop and conclude. You get the pleasure of transforming a negative Nellie or a doubting Thomas into happy, loyal customers who leave singing your praises. Did I mention the part where being able to ask for just about anything within your framework of rapport includes being able to ask your customer to spread the word about how great you are?

It is important to treat every customer with the same respect, expectation and intention that you treat your favorite clients – the ones who keep coming back to appreciate the value you have to offer. However, every once in a while you will find yourself dealing with a customer who cares only about price. Winning him over is a losing game.

Section 3

The price shopper will buy from you one day, then an on-line retailer the next, and then your competitor down the street the day after that. Chasing this kind of customer is like chasing your tail. It hurts when you catch it. The price shoppers are the ones who are more likely to complain about the trivial, and badger you to lower your price still further or to dig out a deeper discount. And they are incapable of recognizing and appreciating the value of your expertise.

Whatever you're selling, there's another guy selling it cheaper. Maybe he's willing to take a loss on that item, or he's going out of business, or the product fell off the back of a truck, or he's paying his workers cash under the table, or he undervalues his services, or it's his way of getting out of having to offer a warranty on his work. The reason is unimportant; someone out there will beat you on price. The fact is that the price shopper will go to the next guy without thinking about you; you're nothing more than a price to him. He'll risk doing business with an unknown quantity to save a few bucks.

The customer who is shopping around for the best price believes that getting the best price is the same as getting the best value. He equates low prices with value. This, I believe, is because he's looking at it the wrong way. He's defining value as saving the physical money in his pocket, and is unable to understand that the invisible values keep more money in his pocket in the long run. He lacks the ability to see past six months or a year. He wants a sofa now, and only wants to pay $399 for it. Well, pretty soon he will need another one, and he will have to spend another $399 or more to replace it. And soon after that, he'll have to replace the second low-quality sofa. A value shopper will spend $1,000 on a sofa because he knows that it comes with a warranty on the frame, as well as stain protection and a different warranty on the cushions, and that it will be a very long time before he needs to replace it. He understands that the craftsmanship that went into designing and building this sofa will also buy him peace of mind, which has its own value price tag.

A man who is willing to spend $1,000 on a piece of furniture will drive right past the stripped-down furniture mart until he finds a place worthy of his investment.

Exceptional Care for Your Valued Client

Interestingly enough, I have a friend whose parents decided to redo their entire house a few years back, and went to a well-known, up-scale furniture gallery with on-site interior designers to help them make the right decisions for their lifestyle. Unfortunately, my friend's parents had been out driving and visiting the grandkids and looked exactly like they had spent the day in a car with children.

A salesperson took one look at them, made a snarky remark, turned up her nose, turned on her heel, and walked away. They were subsequently ignored for about 20 minutes until they left. This happened 15 years ago, and they still remember it. They refuse to step foot in any branch of this store. This is a perfect example of a salesperson thinking too much of the value of what the business has to offer. At no point in time and under no circumstances is it appropriate to assume you are too good for your customers and then proceed to alienate them.

Treating this couple like king and queen for a day would have been appropriate, whether they were there to get ideas, buy one chair, or refurnish a room.

It is important to qualify your customers before assuming they are price shoppers or value shoppers. The only way to do this is by approaching them with the right intention and expectations so that you can establish a Framework of Rapport. Within that framework you can discover, discreetly, what their spending comfort level is, what they think their needs are, what their needs really are, and what they'd really like to have happen.

You want to pay attention to setting up and maintaining this Framework of Rapport, because within it, and only within it, can you ask your customer to acknowledge the value of your product or service with her pocketbook. Talking your customer into a purchase she is unable to afford and will soon regret creates a negative memory for her, so make sure you respect what you hear and pick up on within the framework.

It is a serious mistake to treat a customer as if you expect them to be a price shopper. It's easier, more efficient, and less time consuming to do

Section 3

this. However, if you've heard the expression "kill them with kindness," you may be able to guess at what I'm going to say next. Treat each and every one of your *"clients"* with the respect due a value shopper, and you will increase the number of value shoppers you attract to your business, and you might even convert a few of those price shoppers. When you treat a customer like just another number in the numbers game, or a price shopper who only pays attention to the bottom line, you alienate them.

To a value shopper, it's the entire experience that counts. Connecting with another human being is important; being able to make eye-contact or small-talk matters. They'll drive right past your competitor and his super sale to do business with you, because they know what to expect, and they know that saving a few dollars rarely saves on the headaches of cheap service.

Competing for the dollars in a price shopper's wallet is a waste of time. Let the other businesses deal with that stress. The real competition is for value shoppers; they're the most valuable prize going.

Remember this when it's time to stand by your prices, your product, the time you take to complete a project, or any of the other factors that add value to what you offer. Confidence in your product and/or service is the key to taking control of a client/customer service encounter and creating a framework of rapport. Value shoppers like their retailers, manufacturers, technicians, service providers, entertainers – the people they do business with – to have such a great product or service that the confidence comes easily, without apologies.

A value shopper appreciates the many details that go into a positive buying experience. They are the ones with whom you can build a loyalty base. They appreciate the personal touch, the comfortable waiting room, the pleasant music, the clean restroom, the lighting, the sound, the way they are greeted, how they are spoken to, and how they are made to feel when they visit you, even if that visit is over the phone or to your web-site. They complain less because they're more willing to give you a break or the benefit of the doubt when things run less smoothly than

Exceptional Care for Your Valued Client

usual because it's in our nature to give our friends a break now and then. All the other factors weigh in when they consider whether an oversight or mistake devalues their overall experience with you.

The value shopper appreciates *Respectful Elegance*. It makes a psychological difference.

Value shoppers will show their appreciation by paying fair to high prices for it. Price shoppers will discount your years of training, the quality of the products and tools you use, and the thought you put into your surroundings, insisting that all that value "*should not*" have anything to do with price. Your service is just a commodity to them; something they can get anywhere. Price shoppers have their place, but they have no loyalty to give, so why bother working to get it? Treat every customer with equal respect, and let the price shoppers fall away.

Within an established Framework of Rapport, you can ask your customer for just about anything. Once you have earned trust, loyalty and respect the old-fashioned way – by proving what you have to offer has genuine value – then you can ask your customer to work with you. You can ask for patience when you are training someone new, forgiveness when you make a mistake, a little extra time when you're working up a quote. You can ask a valued customer to reschedule when you have over-booked, to go along with and actually feel it's appropriate when you have to raise your prices, and even to remain loyal when a competitor offers a tempting coupon.

On the flipside, you can go the extra mile for a valued customer with whom you have an established framework of rapport because you know it will be appreciated. It is safe to give more of yourself and your attention because you know you have their loyalty and support, and it becomes important to you, on a personal and professional level, to show your appreciation for that loyalty.

In preceding chapters I concentrated on individual word choice, body language and behavior. In this chapter, I wanted to incorporate how important the physical environment is in creating a Framework of

Section 3

Rapport, and how invisible values play a role in communicating with your client. The next chapter is devoted to teamwork. If you're the one-and-only owner/operator of your business and exceptional client service seems like a solo effort, I'd like to reassure you that the next chapter will be of value to you, as well.

Exceptional Care for Your Valued Client

Section 3

Section 3 Exercises

The Whole Package: Delivery and Results

Have you ever *caught* someone verbalizing "yes" and physically saying "no"?

This is a common occurrence in conversation, and usually in the customer service experience. For your first exercise, I would like you to identify five circumstances where you observed instances of incongruent articulation in the person's physiology. Watch for the disconnection in the conversation. Focus on the confusion that the message sends, and identify the specific word choice where the incongruence occurs.

This is a powerful exercise when you embrace it and engage the process.

1 _____
_____
_____
_____
_____
_____

2 _____
_____
_____
_____
_____
_____

3 _____
_____
_____
_____
_____
_____

Exceptional Care for Your Valued Client

4 _____
_____
_____
_____
_____

5 _____
_____
_____
_____
_____

For your second exercise, focus on the Framework of rapport you establish with your employees and foster an environment for them to flourish in their own crafting of a new framework.

Help them develop questions that foster that new framework. Point out the importance of expanding their horizons to meet your customers and clients where "they are" in the business relationship, the client experience and the client care extravaganza.

For your third exercise, pay particular attention to the Rapport you are establishing in the physical location of your business. Revisit Chapter 15 and focus on the details described.

Consider having your best clients help you create your environment. After all, they are the ones who can offer valuable feedback because they keep returning to transact business with you.

Their input is priceless.

SECTION 4

The Difference is in the Details

Chapter 16: It takes Time to Deliver Value

Chapter 17: ABCs of Emotion – How Dare You Have an Attitude

Chapter 18: Circling the Situation – Several Alternatives Available

Exercises for Section 4

Exceptional Care for Your Valued Client

Section 4

Chapter 16

It takes Time to Deliver Value

Teamwork among your employees, or the lack thereof, can make or break you. LuAnn has a sister whose recent experience demonstrates the importance of making sure each one of your employees – especially the least service-savvy of the group – is equipped and motivated enough to at least back up the employees who are attuned to meeting and exceeding customer needs.

While planning a large family event that would bring people together from different parts of the country, LuAnn's sister worked with an agent who helped her choose and rent two large campers at the same time. Together they went over the family's needs, their plans, which vehicles offered which amenities, which decisions would incur which expenses, where the hidden perks and drawbacks of each lay, and just about all the pertinent details the two of them could think of that concerned LuAnn's sister. Judging by the result (the decision to rent more than one vehicle), it was a productive and successful arrangement for both parties – especially the agent who invested time and attention to serving her customer.

The day arrived for LuAnn's sister to pick up the campers, and she woke with the task of coordinating a busy schedule foremost on her mind. The rental offices had opened at 8 a.m., and looking at her watch, she figured 8:30 was a smart time to call and find out exactly what time she and a couple of helpers could drive over and get them. Excited to get the official family event underway, she picked up the phone, confirmation information in hand, and dialed.

The young man who answered the phone was either hung-over, woke up on the wrong side of the bed, or had yet to drink his first cup of coffee. Whatever the excuse, he ruined all the hard work the agent before him had put into earning this customer's business and, more importantly, any loyalty she felt. He was unwilling to carry on with the agent's level of service.

Exceptional Care for Your Valued Client

"I don't know," he said, cutting her off with an ill-mannered response. "You'll have to talk to Judy. She will be here at nine. Call back then."

LuAnn's sister put down the phone, stunned and annoyed. Did he really just do that? Did he really just blow her off without any thought for how it felt to be treated so abruptly, or consideration for her need to have the information she asked for? Who was this Judy person and why did she have to wait for her? She was spending a lot of money with this company, and this is the treatment she got? Annoyance stewed into anger as the clock ticked down to 9 a.m., and stayed with her for a long time.

LuAnn had the dubious honor of being a witness to her sister's reaction, and she went with her to pick up the campers.

You can bet there were few smiles to go around when she and her family picked up the vehicles.

If the young man on the phone had been even the least bit helpful, offered to find the information himself, or even offered to have this Judy person return the phone call when she got in, LuAnn's sister would have had an entirely different story to tell, one that included how great the campers were, how easy the process of renting them was, and the assurance she would book with them again in the future, as well as a recommendation for others to use their services.

One bad apple spoiled the barrel, and LuAnn's sister is looking at other companies for her business next year.

"When you are faced with completing a coworker's job like this, there are better ways to handle that person's client. At a minimum, a concerned tone and a promise to have 'Judy' call the moment she arrived was in order. Up from minimum would be figuring out the answer yourself, with a tone of voice that clearly states 'I'm so happy to be able to do this for you myself.'" LuAnn exhorts, and emphasizes the need for empowered individuals who appreciate the benefits of functioning like a team.

Section 4

"Professionalism means being able to carry the ball when it has been passed to you, to offer a consistent or even better level of customer service than the person before you. It requires the ability to act on your own, like this is your customer and her happiness depends on you." After all, every customer will reflect how they have been treated by your business, regardless of who they have contact with.

If the person answering the phone in the morning is unable to answer questions, he had better know how to take messages in a way that instills confidence.

"The 'unempowered' or disempowered employee costs you money! When he says 'I don't know, that's someone else's job,' or 'I don't know, that's just the way we do it,' or any other combination of words that send the same message of being unwilling and unable to help, he takes money out of your wallet and gives it to your competition.

Your customer wants to work with the capable and competent; and only a professional, empowered employee can make that impression."

"If you tell me to call back, I'll likely call someone else," LuAnn continues. "Forget for a minute how rude it is to tell a customer to call back, and the fact that she neither knew nor cared who this Judy person was. This person just missed a chance to make my sister fall *in love with him and his service*, to give his name and establish his own rapport with someone who booked TWO campers at the same time. He cost himself something, cost the original agent a lot of time and energy, and cost the company my sister's business next year. He also missed a chance to capture her phone number and permission to call her – about that day's business and future opportunities to do business. Marketing 101, people."

Here we go again with the point that we continue to make; it is extremely important to understand the following:

Starting a business is about opening the doors and getting people to come in.

Exceptional Care for Your Valued Client

Staying in business is about pleasing those people enough that they will want to come back in, again and again.

Remember it is far easier to keep clients, then it is to go out and find new ones.

If you want their money, you need to learn how to serve them in a way in which they want to be served. You may have 15 people on your staff; skilled in pleasing the customer with professional behavior and thoughtful treatment, yet if you let the one person who has a bad attitude or has no clue there is a difference between how you say good morning with a smile on your face and how you say it with no eye contact, then you are going to have problems.

Every single person in your organization must have the power and ability to back up every other single person in your organization, so your customer notices no difference between working with one over the other. The goal is a seamless experience for the customer, regardless of how many hands pitch in to take the process from beginning to end.

LuAnn and I, in our separate yet similar industries, have been hearing complaints for years now about how customer service standards seem to be getting lower and lower across the board. We discuss the dilemma with colleagues and business associates in networking meetings, share horror stories over coffee with friends, even post comments on social networking sites including Facebook – like so many people today, lamenting at the appalling state of affairs in the world today. This entire book is dedicated to waking up the business owner and exceptional care representatives by demonstrating the why's and wherefore's – and especially the how's – of elevating that standard of service back to a place of pride and effectiveness. The goal must be providing Exceptional Care for Your Valued Client, a standard higher than what is called customer service in the 21st century.

What do you think the most common complaint about customer service is? A sullen or confrontational attitude? Low-brow use of language? Is it the person behind the counter who is carrying on a conversation with

Section 4

someone else, verbally or via text, while they're helping you?

Here's one to consider: Increasingly, consumers are complaining about businesses that promise the moon and the stars to new customers, and once they have that target consumer in their grips and the contract signed, the customer service goes to pot.

Businesses are failing their existing customers, the people they're hoping to be valued clients.

Why do you think one company can woo customers away from another so easily? It's because businesses that capture the competition's customer know people want to feel special, wanted, desired, and even lucky; and that who they're currently with is taking them for granted.

Who likes feeling that their business is taken for granted?

The great failing comes with an attitude of forgetfulness once that consumer has been caught. Creating irresistible promotions, carefully constructing an image to attract new customers, and spending fantastic amounts of money to woo these customers away from the competition is a fool's errand unless you are prepared to keep up the love affair through the entire relationship, and put in the effort a long-term relationship requires to thrive.

Attraction, flirtation, the rush of exhilaration when the dance begins, the boost to the ego that mutual desire brings along with it... wooing a client is an act of enticement that some of us are very, very good at. However, without substance to back up your silver-tongued promises that delight, can fizzle and turn sour if you neglect to nurture it.

If you want to keep your customers interested in you, and you alone, you have to be both willing and able to do the hard work, to follow through on promises made and to be able to prove yourself reliable and trustworthy over the long haul. Each member of your team, from the top down through the ranks, must be invested in the same goal: Providing Exceptional Care for the Valued Client. Give your valued client a reason

Exceptional Care for Your Valued Client

to stay, and she will stay. Give her a reason to leave, and she will leave. Neglect, rudeness, broken promises, and being made ineligible for the same or comparable perks the new client gets will turn your client on her heel, and she will walk right into the waiting arms of someone else.

The Framework of Rapport you have with your employees; and they have with each other is the key to creating and maintaining a team that runs like a well-oiled machine.

LuAnn relies heavily on the teams that back her up, whether they're her own people or her vendors – which are carefully chosen for their ability to provide exceptional care for her, their valued client. Her years in hotel management made the importance of teamwork all the way down the line abundantly clear, especially on one occasion when she needed to think out of the box to accommodate a client. Without the team of empowered individuals behind her, she would have been unable to present the solution she came up with to her customer.

At one point in her career, LuAnn worked for a hotel in the city of Rochester, Minnesota, which happens to be the home of the Mayo Clinic. Patients and their family members would fly in the night or a few nights before an appointment at the Mayo Clinic and stay at one of the hotels in the area, including LuAnn's, on a very regular basis. LuAnn remembers one patient clearly, and fondly, because the woman challenged her customer service skills like no other had before her.

"On an evening when I was working at the front desk, a customer arrived who had been traveling something like 18 or 20 hours. She had a reservation with us, however we had overbooked, as hotels do in order to survive the typical 10 percent cancellation/no-show rate for booking rooms. We had overbooked, and there were no rooms available for this woman," LuAnn recalls.

"This happens every once in a while, and the common solution is to find another hotel nearby for the customer and make arrangements for him or her to stay there until a room becomes available at your own hotel."

Section 4

LuAnn offered to arrange accommodations and transportation for the woman in front of her; however, the 18 or 20 hours of traveling had taken its toll. The woman had a very strong reaction. "I'm sick and I'm tired," she said angrily, "and I refuse to take one more step!"

She literally refused to take one more step.

That was all there was to it. She refused to budge. She was angry she had a reservation but no room; she was angry she was sick and there was nothing anyone could do about it that night; and she was angry that what she thought had been the end of a wearying day looked to have no actual end in sight. She was immovable.

"I could appreciate how she felt," LuAnn says, knowing how bad a bad day can make you feel, even when you're unhealthy and close to home. "So I said, 'let me take a second and figure this out' so that I could step away from the situation and consider the possibilities. Rather than trying to come up with a way to convince her to leave, which was probably going to be impossible, I focused on how I could manage to help her stay. That's what she was really asking for under all the anger and the stubborn refusal to move on. She was saying 'please help me.'"

Because LuAnn redirected her purpose to accommodating rather than getting rid of the woman, she was able to return to the desk within a few minutes to begin again with "Can I offer you this...?"

LuAnn asked the woman to be patient for 45 minutes to an hour while the hotel staff turned a small conference room into a sleeping room. "It is right across the hall from a bathroom. We will bring in a roll-away bed, lamps, and everything you need to be comfortable for the night. Tomorrow we will have a regular room available for you and we will move you right over, so this is just for one night only. What do you think?"

The woman took it.

What happened next took cooperation from the entire staff as they worked quickly and diligently to transform a cold conference space into

Exceptional Care for Your Valued Client

a warm, welcoming sleeping room. The woman slept comfortably for the night, moved into another room the next day, and wrapped up her experience at the hotel with the knowledge that she had been important enough for LuAnn to listen to her and take whatever extra steps were needed to make her happy.

In typical LuAnn fashion, she herself walked away from the experience crediting the success to the team that backed her up: It took willing and able individuals from all over the hotel, from housekeeping, room service, maintenance, just about everywhere, to take their own steps outside the rules and routines to set the room up with furnishings, linens, towels, food, a phone, and the rest of the amenities necessary to making the client feel at home.

When pushed to pat herself on the back, LuAnn says, "It all comes down to you. Your management style sets the example. Your employees are a reflection of you and your attention to detail, quality, deadlines and all the other things that make your business work. They are your most important asset, your most important resource, your front line to the customers.

The way you treat your employees is directly reflected in the way they treat your customers. When you are willing to bend over backwards and do what it takes to provide exceptional care for your valued clients, you will find your employees following your lead and doing the same thing as naturally as breathing. I had the vision: A conference room transformed into a comfortable sleeping room. My crew took that vision and built it. They are the ones who brought in the pieces and made it real."

LuAnn's employees were empowered to take her vision and figure out how to make it happen. They rolled up their sleeves and did it quickly and with enthusiasm, with no time or inclination to say "that's not my job."

Did you recognize the importance of what LuAnn is saying there? "Your employees are a reflection of you." "They are your most important asset." "The way you treat your employees is… the way they treat your customers." "You will find your employees following your lead… as naturally as breathing."

Section 4

LuAnn believes very strongly in the power of empowered employees, and she also believes in the power of creating a sense of community within your business, among your empowered employees. We've been calling it teamwork, and I think either word works; teams function best when they have a sense of community, communities function best when the whole community is in it together – like a team.

"Creating that environment inside your business is the best way to ensure the individuals who work there will have each others' back. When there's a sense of community, there's a kind of pleasure that goes along with doing what's best for the community," LuAnn points out.

I agree. A sale may be Sarah's, but the customer belongs to the group, so you all behave with professionalism and lend a helping hand when called on. Next time, the sale may be yours, and the atmosphere you helped create will help you close that sale.

"If you think about it," LuAnn says, "businesses of every size and shape function like a hotel. Everyone has separate jobs, and they are all necessary. If you're missing equipment or people, or the right attitude, how will we all get together and do the job for the customer?"

At the hotel, LuAnn set the tone for how to treat the customer. She set the customer's expectations at a certain level, and trusted that the teams and community behind her, supporting her, would continue to keep that bar elevated. That tone and that standard can be broken anywhere down the line, and the more people you have in the mix, the more vigilant you have to be about how you train and lead them, as a group and as individuals.

What if LuAnn made a bad impression, or set a tone that grated on the customer's nerves? What if LuAnn made a good impression, but the next person to talk to the customer was in a sour mood and disrupted the experience? How do you prevent a chain reaction that goes from good to bad to worse when someone drops the ball?

LuAnn teaches that empowering employees to make a difference means empowering them to set the chain in another direction. Sometimes a

Exceptional Care for Your Valued Client

customer needs to be rescued from a salesperson having a bad morning. A team-mate can make all the difference by joining the group, taking over, or just making sure that the next step in the process is back on track and better for the customer. We all have bad days. Team-mates help us refocus.

Every once in a while you will come across a customer who, for reasons beyond your understanding, has taken a strong disliking to you. You may remind him of a mean neighbor who ran over his bike when he was a child. Your haircut, or the cut of your blazer, or the cut of your jib may bug him. Maybe your voice sets her teeth on edge, or she just broke up with a jerk with the same name, or she's estranged from a sister who wears the same perfume.

This is when you will be grateful for working in a community of team-mates you can rely on. If you can, excuse yourself by offering to find a team-mate who you deliberately describe as 'better informed' or 'more familiar with' the product or service so the customer feels special. Maintain your smile and your professionalism, and move on to the next customer. Remember to have your your team-mate's back when she runs across the customer who confuses her with the teacher who failed her both semesters of freshman year for conjugating French words all incorrectly.

If you can create a sense of community among your employees, your co-workers; or whoever helps you serve the customer; you can strengthen that well-oiled machine: *your business!*

A leader leads by example. If you want your employees to work together as a team of people who treat the customer with respect, you have to demonstrate it to your employees first. Show them twice: First and foremost by how you treat your staff, then, of course, how you treat the customer.

If you manage a restaurant, treat your wait staff like the entrepreneurs that they are and the customers will do the same. Treat them like servants, and your customers will look down their noses at you, your servers, and the whole dining experience. When you treat your employees well at the back of the house, they treat your paying customers well at the front of the house. It's a very simple concept, and

Section 4

I keep repeating it. I'm hoping it will sink in, because there's a reason customer service is at an all-time low, and it begins with the people who train the people who serve the customers.

If you want to eliminate the bad attitude creeping into your customer service staff, or the one that walked in with the new guy, TEACH the right way to do it. Have you heard those powerful and empowering words of Mahatma Gandhi, "Be the change you want to see in the world"? Well, be the change you want to see in your *Exceptional Care*. Build a Framework of Rapport and build a community within it where each individual can ask their team-mates anything, and then watch how that team begins to make your customers feel like they are a part of your community, too. It's interesting and exciting to see how it all rolls forward, with dignity, clarity, respect, expectations of good, and a genuine interest in serving the customer all combining to build your business for you over the years.

Be the change, and begin with clarity.

We have talked at length about word choice and empowering versus disempowering ways to communicate with customers. We've discussed the importance of congruency, and the idea of building a framework of rapport that includes words, demeanor and physical surroundings.

LuAnn has shared excellent examples of how a team-mate can cost you business, what it means to have a community of people back you up at work, and how important leadership is in determining the kind of Exceptional Client Care your business has to offer. All of these factors are significant and important, and now that you have them in your possession, it's time to get down to the nitty-gritty of the No. 1 complaint the general public have with today's customer service:

Attitude.

How do you turn it around to work for you? Let's find out. In the next few chapters I'm going to get right down to the core of the issue. Where does the attitude come from, and how do you change it?

Exceptional Care for Your Valued Client

Section 4

Chapter 17

The ABCs of Emotions
How Dare You Have an Attitude?

This chapter is dedicated to the fact: *there are thoughts and beliefs behind behavior.*

Emotions manifest in what we commonly call "attitudes." Positive emotions show up as a result of "good attitudes", while negative emotions come from "bad attitudes." Bad attitudes are a plague in today's world of customer service, and they happen on both sides of the counter. It's your job to figure out how to eliminate bad attitudes on your side, and at least manage negativity that shows up on your customer's side.

Some thoughts seem to be written on the face of the thinker. You may find one or two of the following translations familiar:

Slight roll of the eyes or muffled sigh of impatience: I'm minding my own business; I wish she'd mind hers.

Blank face, no eye contact and tired "uh-huh": I'm here to ring up your groceries; who cares if your cat likes this food more than the last kind you bought?

Frozen smile and immediate return to canned greeting: I see a million of you people come through here every day; you really think I'm going to remember your face, let alone your name?

Instructions spoken in a mumble directed down at the desk or up at the wall behind the customer: I just want to keep my head down and get through this day; if I fade away into the background, maybe everyone will leave me alone?

Eyes flicking around, knee shaking or fingernail-biting, distracted speech

Exceptional Care for Your Valued Client

or incomplete sentences: Payday is tomorrow and I only have enough for some of my bills. Do I pay the electric bill or get groceries?

Obviously "on show" but attention on the other side of the room: What's that cute guy in the warehouse doing up here? Do I have something in my teeth?

Puffed up chest, condescending tone, bored or sneering expression: How dare this jerk question me in front of my supervisor? My little sister knows more about this laptop than he ever will. He needs to shut up and buy it and stop bothering me.

Rushed speech and failure to acknowledge a possible need to slow down or repeat instructions: This really is a simple process; why do I have to keep explaining myself over and over to this person? Can we just print out the instructions and hang them on the wall already? This is lame.

Each of the above examples can be chalked up to an excusable lapse when it happens once in a blue moon. If an otherwise friendly and attentive person exhibits one or two of these behaviors occasionally, it's called being human. The problem arises when these behaviors are the norm. Then they get swathed with the label "bad attitude" or "poor service" and your reputation suffers.

Where do habitual, seemingly unshakeable bad attitudes come from, and why do they have to consume your day when all you're wanting to do is run a business?

"Business should not be personal," you say. I've heard this one a time or two. Listen to yourself allowing "should" and "not" to confuse the truth. Business IS personal. You do business with persons. Even if you do business with corporations and/or governments, you interact with a person or persons somewhere along the line. Deny it all you want, and then when you're done, pay attention.

In a nutshell, attitudes come from how a person views a situation or event. Shakespeare summed it up pretty eloquently in Hamlet, Act 2,

Section 4

Scene 2: "...there is nothing either good or bad, but thinking makes it so." Rosencrantz and Guildenstern thought Denmark was a pretty cool place to hang out, but Hamlet thought Denmark a prison. In other words, things and events are just things and events; our pre-conceived ideas determine our attitudes about them.

Customer service is a craft that needs to be honed like any other. It requires a skill-set that enables you to interact successfully with your customers. The fundamental ingredients begin and end with them feeling respected, attended to, and appreciated. For some of us, this ability comes smoothly and easily; natural charm is a part of our basic toolkit. For others, forcing a smile for a stranger is just that: Forcing a smile for a stranger. It feels unnatural, fake, and dishonest.

How, then, can you exhibit genuine congruence of words, thoughts and behaviors when you feel like you are forcing yourself to fake it? There is only one answer: You have to get past whatever is holding you back from being genuine so that there's no need to fake anything.

Word choice is the key to providing Exceptional Care for your valued client, and to be successful you have to be able to think clearly, with the customer's best interests in mind, in order to make the best word choices.

A good attitude produces good thoughts, which produce good word choices. Pretty simple, right? A bad attitude may produce a good word choice from a handy list of word choices, but that negativity will come through and ruin the effect. Consider rushed speech, lack of eye contact, part of the body turned away from the customer, being distracted by a cell-phone or the next task at hand, talking to a co-worker while serving a customer, and lack of animation on the speaker's face – all subliminal cues to the customer that she is an inconvenience and a waste of time. Without congruence of attitude with word choice, there's no convincing her otherwise.

In order to make any successful changes on the outside, you must examine where your feelings come from on the inside. Negative behavior

Exceptional Care for Your Valued Client

and bad attitudes have a source. So, let's get to the source. Let's take a look at where attitudes come from and what it takes to change them. The key is to understand how and why we have control over how we feel about any given situation, and use that understanding to create positive change. Fortunately, it turns out that it's as easy as A-B-C.

In the 1950's Dr. Albert Ellis developed a breakthrough concept, widely known today as Rational Emotive Therapy, to explain the phenomena I'm referring to. You may have heard of it, and you may be familiar with how it works.

Dr. Ellis called it the ABCs of Emotion, and this is how it breaks down:

- A refers to the event that took place
- B refers to your thoughts about the event, which encapsulates your beliefs, values and opinions
- C refers to your feelings about the event, or your emotional response.

A leads to B, which leads to C. C is a result of B. B traps you in your unsuccessful mind-set or bad attitude, and C is the resulting emotional response. The key to moving toward a new emotional response, is Disputing the thoughts and beliefs about your event.

The event just is. It is beyond your control. It happened or is happening to you. Your beliefs about the event dictate your feelings about the event. The key to moving toward a new emotional response, is Disputing the thoughts and beliefs you have about your event.

In the 1970s, Dr. Maxie Maultsby rounded out the ABCs with a D and an E. He took Dr. Ellis' concept a step further and hypothesized that if you go back to B and identify the faulty or disempowering thinking that leads to strong negative emotions, then you can change that thinking and thereby change the emotions that manifest as a result of how you interpret A, the event. He labeled this process D for Disputing the Thoughts. The new, more empowered emotions he labeled E.

Section 4

This is the process of re-education we talked about earlier, and here is the classic example of the ABCs of Emotion that I used in my first book, Remember the Ice and Other Paradigm Shifts. It clearly demonstrates the entire concept in a nutshell.

A: A man is laid off from work. That's the event. There is nothing he can do about it. It just happened.

B: He has been raised to believe that a man without a job is a slacker, a loser, and a burden on society. He thinks he has lost his ability to earn the money needs to pay the bills and feed his children. In his opinion, he is less than a man because he no longer has a job.

C: He is deeply shaken. He feels depressed. His shame turns his self-esteem to rubble. He is anxious and afraid that he will be unable to pay his bills and his children will starve.

The only way for this man to find his way out of this hopeless attitude of failure and self-loathing is for him to progress through D and E.

D requires the man to re-examine B, his thoughts, about A, the event. First, does being laid off from one job mean he will be a burden on society for the rest of his life? No. Does being laid off from one job mean he has lost the skills and talents he brought to the job in the first place, or the skills and talents he acquired while working there? No.

He has a choice. He can choose how he thinks about being laid off, and what he thinks about being laid off. What if I told this man that being laid off was a golden opportunity to pursue another line of work within his career, or a whole new career, and that if he still had that job he would be unable to do so? His thoughts about the event would begin to change. He would be able to start looking at it as a gateway to new opportunity, rather than as the end of all opportunity.

Once he changes his perspective, how he then feels about being laid off also changes dramatically. Suddenly, he is filled with hope, open to new ideas, and able to recognize the different opportunities that begin to come his way.

Exceptional Care for Your Valued Client

The toughest and most challenging part of making that transition to E, the empowered emotions, is honestly and thoroughly examining your thoughts and beliefs about an event.

When I practice and teach the ABCs of Emotion, I focus on word choice as the key to getting from B and C to D and E. I believe the key to rational self-counseling is empowering self-talk, and empowering self-talk only occurs after you have eliminated disempowering words from your vocabulary.

Let's apply this to a few customer service situations.

Zack and the Lake

- A: A young man, Zack, has to work on the Fourth of July while his friends go to the lake for the day. That's the event. There is nothing he can do about it.

- B: Zack believes that he is young and "should" be having fun, that he is entitled to enjoy the holiday with everyone else, and that he is missing out on what he deserves. He believes his boss is greedy for staying open on a holiday, and unreasonable for expecting him to work a full shift, unless business is slow. He resents being at the restaurant, he resents his boss, and he resents the customers who keep coming in to be served. He starts grousing to the kitchen staff about the customers. "Are they too lazy to stay home and barbecue like everyone else? Did they miss the memo that this is a holiday and WE have a right to a day off, too?!? Why do they have to bring their grubby little kids and is anyone going to tell them how stupid they all look in matching red, white and blue?" He starts grousing at the kitchen staff.

- C: Zack is angry. He feels irritated, impatient, and resentful, and it shows.

Zack knows he needs to plaster a smile on his face when he stands at each table to interact with the customers, but no one is fooled. The only way for him to redeem himself, revert to his usual outgoing personality,

Section 4

and make the most of the event that is beyond his control (being at work instead of at the lake), is to look at B, his thoughts and attitude about having to work on a holiday so that he can progress through D and E.

- D: Zack steps outside for a minute on his break. Having been through one of my Remember the Ice seminars, he decides to take a good look at B and identify whether his beliefs about working on a holiday make sense. Zack likes his job well enough, usually. The atmosphere is fun, he considers his co-workers his friends, the pay is okay and people generally tip well. In fact, they're pretty generous when Zack is on his game. He even has a small following of regulars who request his section when they come in to dine. Truth be told, taking the day off and running up to the lake would have hit him hard in the pocketbook. When he thinks about the money he is making and the fact that he likes his job and his co-workers, he can feel a shift in his feelings. "If the lake is out of the question, I might as well enjoy where I am," he decides. He admits to himself that he really wanted to be waterskiing, and then he lets it go. There is nothing he can do about being at work instead of on the water, so he decides to make sure he's more assertive about saying no to his boss on the next holiday, and goes back inside ready to be his usual happy, entertaining self.

- E: He feels lucky to have a job he likes and a boss who gives him extra opportunities to earn money. It's the Fourth of July, and those kids in there could probably use a scoop of ice cream and a balloon from the front counter.

Zack changed his thoughts (D) about having to work (A), which immediately freed him emotionally to feel differently (E). He went back to his customers with a sense of enjoyment and an instinct for adding the little extras that make the difference between hum-drum service and exceptional care.

Tamera and her Temerity

- A: Tamera has a job that is tedious and repetitive. She answers phones and fills out paperwork all day. She is a single mother who also supports

Exceptional Care for Your Valued Client

her own mother. She is an hourly employee, working full-time, and taking a day off to find a more suitable job that she enjoys is out of the question. That is the event. There is nothing she can do about it at this time.

- B: Tamera went to college, almost graduated, and has proven before that she can do more and contribute more than this job allows. She believes that the job is beneath her. She believes that she compromised and settled on a job that fails to challenge her because no other jobs were available. She believes she must be dependable and reliable; taking a risk to find a job that fulfills her would be selfish and impractical. She also believes; at her age she should be much further along in a successful career.

- C: Tamera has lost respect for herself. She feels ashamed and embarrassed that she is in her thirties and doing tasks that remind her of her first job as a teenager. Most days she can barely bring herself to make eye contact with customers, especially if they're her age and dress better. Sometimes, she shuts them out and just goes through the motions because it is too painful to see the disdain she expects to find in their faces. She is neither patient nor impatient when she helps them fill out their paperwork; she answers questions competently and clearly, but remains impersonal. Tamera is miserable.

- D: Tamera thinks about the fact that she went to college and has proven she is capable of a lot more than she has shown. She realizes this is something to be proud of. For that matter, so is raising children on her own and taking care of her mother. She can hold her head high for that, at least, and that is quite a lot. She is indeed dependable and reliable, and begins to think that part of being dependable and reliable includes taking the right risks for a better future. She wants to be further along in her career, so all she needs to do is identify the next step she wants to take and turn this position into a stepping stone to get her there. Tamera decides to embrace the opportunities she has in this job to start breaking out of her shell and let go of the fears that hold her back. Is it possible that what her supervisor says is true, that if she smiles and makes eye contact with the customers then she and they will enjoy the process that much more?

Section 4

- E: Instantly, Tamera feels better. Cheerful. Proud of herself; empowered; hopeful.

No longer ashamed of her job or herself, she finds herself excited to greet the next person and practice the customer service skills she will need in the job she has decided to aim for. The smile on her face is so big and so emphatic, she almost makes herself laugh. Suddenly, the dreary, run-down atmosphere seems to come alive, and each person waiting in line to fill out paperwork can feel it; Tamera's attitude is contagious.

Hank and the Hardware Store

- A: Hank's hardware store is failing. Last year a big-box hardware store opened up five miles away. Sales began to drop off slowly at first, and then plummeted suddenly. The big-box hardware store is now his competition, and yet he has neither the budget nor the inventory to compete. He has one card up his sleeve; he can provide a level of personal service and friendly atmosphere that mega-stores are unable to achieve. He can close his doors, or he can focus on providing the best customer service in town. That choice is the event.

- B: Hank learned everything about the hardware business from his father, the original owner. He was brought up believing, among other things, that real hardware stores are for real men; they're supposed to smell like tools and paint and sawdust, and they're supposed to be safe places where husbands can hide out from their wives on the weekend. He was brought up believing men are responsible for the maintenance and repairs around the house and women are responsible for the cooking and cleaning and child-rearing. He believes in the sanctity of the hardware store as a "man's world." He believes men appreciate the raw, nuts-and-bolts of a no-frills environment, and that cleaning up, fixing up and painting up the store is a waste of time and money. He believes that making his hardware store attractive to women as well as men would be tantamount to letting girls into the clubhouse: Unthinkable.

Exceptional Care for Your Valued Client

- C: Hank feels defeated. He feels like his way of life is ending. He is depressed; his father's legacy will end with him. He feels angry and resentful; the big-box hardware store is robbing him of his livelihood and his chance to pass the business on to his own son and business partner, Hank Jr. If his business closes, he will lose the place where customers who turned into friends decades ago come in to hang out and shoot the breeze. He fears the loss of his identity, his income, and his purpose. The weight of this is almost too much to bear. He barely acknowledges customers who walk through the door. He growls at children and dismisses questions with a half-sneer. He is afraid to be helpful; he is afraid to get attached. He fiddles with tools and locks himself in the office, leaving it to his employee to give the advice Hank used to be famous for.

- D: Hank's son comes into the store on his off-day and pulls up a chair up to sit across from his father. "It's time to talk, dad," he says. "We need to make some changes around here, or shut the doors for good. I know it's going to be hard, but if you would just listen to me, you might like what I have to say. I know how we can compete with that mega-store." Hank listens to his son extol the virtues of making the hardware store women-friendly, of reorganizing and color-coding the shelves, of giving the place a face-lift with fresh paint, modern lighting and flowers, of adding a rack of interior design magazines and basic do-it-yourself books, of adding a line of eco-friendly products and custom hardware lines for the DIY couples who are moving into the neighborhood. What he hears is his son getting excited about the store for the first time since he was a kid.

Hank thinks about losing the legacy he and his father worked so hard to establish, and he thinks about how he used to get excited about trying new things for the business before he got settled in his ways. Hank starts to think about having to change the way he's done things for so long, and how it might be nice to have young people coming into his store again, and how there are a lot more single moms out there now than there were in his day, and that they have every bit the same need – and right – to know how to work on their homes as anyone else. He used to see himself as a neighborhood guru of sorts,

Section 4

the go-to-guy for all manner of fix-it advice over a cup of Joe, and every man's friend. That was the identity he loved the most.

His mind starts ticking, and he interrupts his son.

"Junior, do you think any of these girls out there would want to learn how to hang shelves from an old man like me?"

"You mean, like take classes from you?"

"Yeah, I guess that's what I mean,"

- E: Hank's heart is thumping; this is the first new, exciting idea he'd had in a long time.

He and his son start writing down a list of classes to offer, and by mid-morning Hank is out on the floor, socializing with the customers and mapping out changes with the employees. He is ready to start the next chapter in the life of the store, and knows with a secret thrill that what he can offer his customers by way of small-town, friendly, personal service is far and away superior to what his competition can offer. There is no way they can stop him now.

Did these trips through the re-education process for Zack, Tamera and Hank look familiar? Did they make sense? Changing your beliefs about what an event means to you is going to drag you through cognitive-emotive dissonance, just as it did them. They had to feel their way through their thoughts and beliefs before they could change their feelings and find the most successful attitudes of gratitude, hope and helpfulness. Remember how I emphasized the importance of intention in previous chapters? The fundamental intentions behind all *Exceptional Care*, if you think about it, are gratitude, hope and helpfulness.

If you are struggling with finding the right motivation to snap yourself or an employee out of a bad attitude or a poor customer service habit, even after using the word choice and physiology tools I've given you, you may want to dig a little deeper and see if there is a philosophy buried

Exceptional Care for Your Valued Client

behind the behavior. Once you identify the root cause of a negative belief, you can begin to reframe it in your mind, re-examine what you think about whatever is going on, and rebuild an emotional context for the experience. It is a truly liberating and empowering process. It is rarely short of life-changing.

Now that you have some insight into the ABCs of the emotions we deal with every day, I'd like to introduce you to something I call "Circling the Situation." You know the old adage, "there are two sides to every story"? I beg to differ. To my way of thinking, there are no sides. There are as many points of view as there are people viewing, and that multiplies when those people shift even slightly one way or the other. In the next chapter we're going to look at the advantages of being able to see an event from multiple angles – including your customer's.

Section 4

Chapter 18

Circling the Situation to Avoid Circling the Drain

Have you ever felt blind-sided by an extreme reaction of anger or frustration from a customer? Has anyone dissolved into tears in front of you? It can be a frightening experience that leaves you feeling helpless in the face of such strong emotions. You can almost feel yourself circling the drain; you're in a vortex that spins and spins, and finding a graceful exit eludes you.

If you want to stop circling the drain, start circling the situation instead.

I use the ABCs of emotion as the foundation for my deepest belief about shifting personal attitudes – yours and your customer's. I call it "Circling the Situation." It helps you detach yourself emotionally while maintaining a balanced perspective of what's going on.

In the late 1970s, after graduate school and a few years in private practice, I took a position with Union County Counseling Services, the local Community Mental Health Agency in Anna, Illinois, where I used Rational Behavior Therapy and the tools of Rational Self-Counseling to serve my clients.

I had given a lot of thought to how I set up my office. I wanted it to reflect my beliefs, and to serve as an environment for open communication and steady growth. First and foremost, I made sure to include an area with comfortable seats that was separate from my work desk. If I was going to help the people who came to me, I wanted them to feel at ease and to understand even on a subconscious level that I was in the trenches with them, as opposed to making suggestions from the other side of some cold desk that put me in a different physical space.

There was enough room for a coffee table within the cozy sitting area, and indeed a nice rectangular one was offered for my use. Yet, I rejected it based on the shape; rectangles have sides. I refused to give the

Exceptional Care for Your Valued Client

appearance that I sat "on the other side" from my clients and most importantly, I wanted to break down the belief that issues have sides in the first place.

We approach the issues in our lives from our unique perspectives. To say that an issue has sides is to limit possibilities. Sides never overlap, never meet in the middle, and never have more than a few dimensions. Human situations – human issues – are complex. Perspectives do overlap, overshadow, bend, twist, meet in the middle then diverge radically. And they have unlimited dimensions.

Rather than bring a rectangle into the space, I fashioned a coffee table out of the top of a round cable wheel. It was the perfect shape for explaining what I mean by circling a situation. Having no sides, the table enforced my belief that there are no sides to the issues that confront us, wrong or otherwise; there are just facts and the perspectives from which we examine them.

Imagine an object at the center of a wheel. If the wheel has eight spokes and you stand at the first one and look at the object in the center, you will see the sides of it that faces you. If you move to the second spoke, more of the object will be revealed to you, while some of it will move out of sight. Move again to the next spoke, and you will have yet another, slightly different perspective. Circling the object reveals its different aspects to you; you see its qualities according to your point of view.

It's important to note that I use a circle here because circles have no sides, and neither do facts. I repeat: Circles have no sides, and neither do facts.

The same is true for any fact, issue, or idea. As I demonstrated with the stories in the previous chapter, changing your opinion is as easy as shifting your point of view. Even a slight change in perspective can lead to huge rewards. When you develop the skill to mentally circle a situation, and see where your customer is coming from, you open yourself up to endless possibilities. You gift yourself with the insight to

Section 4

choose words and solutions that resonate with your customer and produce the results you're both looking for.

A customer who storms into your place of business looking for a confrontation is likely to elicit strong reactions. He is on one side, you are on the other. It's a fight to assert which side is right, and no one ends up winning. Or you can take a breath, diplomatically discover the facts about the event that has upset him, and figure out what thoughts and beliefs are causing the emotions that have manifested in threatening behavior.

You delivered 10,000 fliers hot off the presses this morning for an event at your customer Jacob's nightclub. There is a misprint. The date is wrong. Jacob is furious. He signed off on the proof, without catching the mistake. You have his signature on the proof in his file, within arm's reach. He knows this, and it makes him angrier still. He is angry at himself, but the anger is no less upsetting because of that fact. In his mind it is only fair that you pay for the mistake since your people failed to catch it; anyone with a calendar would have known it was wrong, and a true professional, he insists, would have caught it, which, he says, makes you an amateur without the ability to think for yourself and correct the mistake.

On top of that, Jacob has already decided that you will be unable to run a fresh set of fliers in time for him to put them up around town and get them into the hands of his patrons, and he has decided, correctly, that even though he believes the fault is yours, you are under no obligation to fix it for free; legally you're absolved of responsibility.

The emotions and the gesturing and the accusations are many, but the facts are few. Jacob has an event to advertise. Jacob made a mistake. The fliers are useless. Jacob is responsible. Jacob needs new fliers. Jacob wants you to solve the problem.

On the surface, this seems like a two-sided situation. However, there are many ways to look at it, and the more you step around the circle while you look, the more opportunities reveal themselves.

Exceptional Care for Your Valued Client

There's the opportunity to get rid of a troublesome customer, handed to you on a silver platter. Who would blame you for throwing him out? The responsibility was ultimately his, and he's here in your face making your employees uncomfortable and halting productivity.

There's the opportunity to make money. He needs the fliers done and you have the design work programmed into the computer. Correct the date, click the mouse a few times, and they're next in line to print. You can charge him exactly what you charged last time, set-up and design fees included, all with a clear conscience; his signature is right there and even he knows it.

There's the opportunity to solidify a relationship with a client who hosts multiple large-scale, popular events a year, the smaller ones at his bar, and the larger ones at different venues around the city. You can correct the date, click the mouse a few times, and charge him the list price for ink and paper, covering your costs with a little extra for dealing with his anger.

There's the opportunity to solidify the relationship and do a little advertising for the cost of ink and paper at wholesale. Maybe Jacob would be willing to let you add your company name and logo to the flier if you offer to reprint at no charge to him, and have it done in record time.

When you have the facts in your hand you can detach your emotions, open your mind, place the facts in the center of that round table and circle them. Circling the situation allows you to see things from your perspective, to see things from your customer's perspective, and to see multiple solutions with varying degrees of win-win for everyone involved.

With a selection of solutions at hand, you maintain control of the situation. You can choose according to your priorities. Maybe making things right with the customer is worth swallowing the cost of ink and paper so that's what you offer. Maybe swallowing the cost of ink and paper will mean you're unable to make the loan payment for the printer, so you need to offer something else. Maybe linking your name to his on the fliers is worth borrowing money from your brother to make that loan

Section 4

payment. At the heart of everything I teach is the admonishment to pause, breathe, and think.

Think about your word choice. Think about your delivery. Think about where the other person is coming from. Think about the solution that will benefit all parties.

Customer service is an innately human experience. There is no way to disentangle yourself from the emotions humans bring along to the party; only humans can react, adapt, respond and behave appropriately to other humans. That's why it is so important to be able to relate to customers on a human level, let them know you see each one as an individual (even if the individuals blend into one in your mind over time), take the time to interact with each one specifically, and understand that you have to deal with the emotions in front of you in as professional a manner as possible.

You affect your customers on an emotional level when you interact with them professionally, and that effect is even more dramatic when your behavior is less than professional, borderline rude, or downright disrespectful. Be aware that every single time you allow an employee to have a negative attitude with a customer or behave in any unprofessional way; you are stating clearly and emphatically that you share that attitude; that you are unprofessional. Your employees, your team, and your co-workers all reflect on you (and you reflect on them).

Am I asking you to get bogged down in the emotional swamp of an unusually and inappropriately needy customer? No. Circling the situation enables you to sidestep the quagmire and stay focused on the facts while demonstrating respect for the other perspective.

You have a product or service to sell at a reasonable price, and you have the knowledge, experience and integrity to back it up. Now I want you to pander to the customer's emotional needs and figure out what's behind your employee's bad attitude all at the same time? That's all well and good, but who has time for that?

Exceptional Care for Your Valued Client

You do. You must. You must make the time to address the emotional side of business. You can make claims about providing *Exceptional Care* and doing everything in your power to ensure the customer's happiness until you're blue in the face, but there is only one way to make sure you can deliver on that promise. You have to make sure there is genuine congruence of thought, word and action in your customer service interactions, regardless of who is actually working with the customer. You may dislike it, but emotions, and the attitudes that result from emotions, influence the thoughts behind words and actions.

How you and your employees view the work being done and the customer being served has everything to do with the attitude that results. If you know how to take a deep breath and re-adjust perspectives and opinions, you will know how to adjust attitudes.

Preaching about change, preaching about cheerfulness, and preaching about customer service skills without getting to the source of the bad attitude is just filling the room with hot air. If you're lucky, you will end up with a robot that can go through the motions and perform correctly (when you're watching), and you will continue to have customers who feel alienated and undervalued, and inclined to take their business elsewhere.

When you develop the ability to embrace your customer's perspective, to see and experience your business through their eyes, you will be able to instinctively identify what is working and what needs improvement. Along with that ability, comes the insight necessary to evolve and grow in the right direction.

As LuAnn pointed out earlier, angry or upset customers just want you to listen. They're really saying, "Please help me." When you have your back up and listening to an angry customer is the last thing you want to do, that's when you most need to pause, take a breath, detach emotionally, determine the facts, place them in the center of that table in your mind's eye so you can circle them, reach into your Remember the Ice bag of tricks, choose your physiology and your word choice, and wow her with your Exceptional Care for Your Valued Client skills.

Section 4

Before word choice, listening is the most important Exceptional Care tool you can have in your kit. Listening lets you know what goes in the middle of the table; listening allows you to look at the facts through your customer's eyes; listening enables you to feel compassion and to choose words and solutions that please and appease. Listening is a great skill to have. It gives you control over just about every situation. When you're busy listening, your mind is busy defining what is really going on by picking up on the said and the unsaid. Paying attention is the key to communication.

Paying attention also happens to be the key to Exceptional Care. In the next chapter, LuAnn is going to take us through some of the old-fashioned notions of Exceptional Care that never go out of style. If you're into the modern and contemporary revolutions of thought, the ideas that are hot and trendy, consider these gems "vintage." The good stuff always comes back.

Exceptional Care for Your Valued Client

Section 4

Section 4 Exercises

The Difference is in the Details

These three chapters ask you to focus on your team, pay attention to your attitudes about Exceptional Care and remember that there are alternatives to any situation.

In using the ABCs of Emotion, you will gain great insight into how you can take charge of how you feel about circumstances in your life. The key is to exercise your ability to come up with empowering alternatives to your original thoughts about the event.

Identify three different events you responded to with emotional responses, at "C", that you would describe as beyond uncomfortable. Were you quite frustrated? Angry? Irritated? Annoyed?

Pay attention to the thoughts you had about the event and be specific in your recollection. Specificity with your thoughts and attitudes is one of the keys to creating empowering alternatives. Focus on the "(K)notty Words" that permeate your thoughts at "B". When you dispute them in "D" and re-frame your thinking, you will be experiencing a more desirable emotional response at "E".

The homework assignment for the ABCs of Emotions is called Rational Self-Analysis. Dr. Maultsby used this framework to assist thousands of individuals with identifying the faulty or disempowering thinking that led to strong negative emotions; then changing that thinking and thereby changing the emotions that manifest as a result of how they interpreted A, the event.

A: The event: Describe your situation. ....
....
....
....

Exceptional Care for Your Valued Client

B. List your thoughts about your event. Be specific. And remember to list as many as you can recall.

....
....
....
....
....
....
....
....
....
....
....
....
....
....
....
....
....
....
....
....

C. How did you feel about your event "A"?..
....
....

D. Begin to Dispute the original thoughts you had at "B". Be objective in your description of the event as well as the thoughts about the event. Pay attention to the facts. Are your thoughts life preserving? (Sometimes people get really hard on themselves). Are your thoughts helping you accomplish your short or long term goals? Are they helping you to minimize significant conflict with your self or others? If you are able to affirmatively answer 3 out of 5 questions, you are developing some empowering alternatives to your original thinking habits and you are shifting your paradigm.

Welcome to a new emotional response:

Section 4

E: How do you feel about the situation now? ....
....
....
....
....
....
....
....
....
....
....
....
....
....
....

Circling the Situation is all about coming up with new thoughts and alternatives about your event. For this exercise, draw a circle around the "X".

Exceptional Care for Your Valued Client

Pick a starting point on your circle and make a *mark*. This becomes your *"point of view"* of "X", which we will call the situation you are dealing with. If you are in a less than desirable circumstance or situation, you might believe you are stuck with your view.

What if you considered moving 180 degrees around the circle, made another mark, and realized that the view changed?

How many degrees in a circle? Right. 360. What if each degree represents a new *"point of view"* or new empowering alternative thought about your situation? Let's stretch this a little more. There are 60 minutes in each degree. That is 21,600 new alternatives! Wait. How many seconds are in each minute? 60 times 21,600 is 1,296,000.

Identify your situation, and move around the circle and embrace 3 to 5 new points of view. Write them down and develop a plan of action to implement the new ideas.

1. ....
   ....

2. ....
   ....

3. ....
   ....

4. ....
   ....

5. ....
   ....

SECTION 5

Where Do You Go From Here?
Accountability & Action Create the Paradigm

Chapter 19: Old-Fashioned Ideas have New Fangled Appeal

Chapter 20: Remember to Pay it Forward and Do the Next Right Thing

Exercises for Section 5

Exceptional Care for Your Valued Client

Section 5

Chapter 19

Old-Fashioned Ideas have New Fangled Appeal

What we need is an Exceptional Care for your Valued Client revolution.

LuAnn and I agree: We need to overthrow the current system of abuse and neglect and replace it with something radical. How about we throw caution to the wind and do something really crazy? How about we use some of the old-fashioned protocols that have fallen into disuse? That, my friend, is the essence of – and the power behind – every message in this book.

Be clear. Make careful word choices. Demonstrate respect. Make eye contact. Listen. Pay attention. Communicate. Personalize even the briefest interactions. Build connections and foster relationships. Follow through on your promises. Be precise about when and what you can deliver. Take responsibility for your mistakes. Make it right when things go wrong. Offer true value and earn your reputation.

Most of all: Enjoy interacting with your customers and make sure it shows. Check your attitude; overlook theirs. The right attitude in providing Exceptional Care is a healthy mix of gratitude, hope and helpfulness. You want their business, so you have to work for it, even if that means slowing down, repeating yourself, and explaining the obvious to the obtuse. Make them feel delighted to do business with you, delighted enough to tell their friends. Prove that you are the best choice in your industry.

Know that you have to earn your reputation. Know that you have to be vigilant about maintaining it.

Take the new tools you have learned to use in this book and apply them to the old way of doing things. That, my friend, may be the most cutting edge, radical course of action you can take. It will certainly set you apart in today's market. These are more than lessens for surviving in a challenging economy; they are lessens for thriving in any economy.

Exceptional Care for Your Valued Client

Use the funny, quirky old phrases you rarely hear nowadays, like "Please," "May I...?" "Thank you," "You're welcome," "It's our pleasure," "We appreciate your business," and "Please come again." The responses you get will amaze and delight you.

When you're with a customer, behave as if nothing else exists. Their needs are the only ones that concern you. If you have to answer a phone, ask permission from your customer. "I am the only person on duty at the moment. May I answer the phone to take a message?"

Have you ever put any of your employees who handle phone calls on hold so they can learn first-hand what 30 seconds feels like? Try it. Thirty seconds goes by quickly – to everyone but the person on hold. Have you called your business after hours to listen to the outgoing message? Have you given the "on-hold" music and/or advertising reel a full minute of your listening time? In other words, have you put yourself in your customer's shoes to find out how your business comes across when the machines are keeping them occupied?

Role play is a wonderful teaching tool, especially when you are still developing the ability to circle situations. Play the part of the customer and have your staff walk through the process of doing business with you. When you are an actual customer at another business, pay attention to what works so that you can emulate it. Pay attention to what is irritating or annoying you so that you can make sure you eliminate any similar policies or habits in your own business.

When you greet or say good-bye to a customer, use full sentences with plenty of keywords. It feels a little formal at first, but you will get used to it. Formal speech is a good attention-getter, for you and the customer. The act of constructing a formal sentence focuses your attention on what you're saying. Hearing a well-composed sentence focuses the customer's attention on you, and makes a stronger psychological impact.

The average customer walking into your business is usually distracted. They're figuring out whether to push or pull on the handle. They might be engaged in conversation, wondering if they put enough money in

Section 5

the parking meter, or intent on finding what they need quickly and holding a list in their mind. It takes several words to get their attention.

When a customer service person says a quick "Hello" or "Good morning," the customer hears "blah-blah" or "blah blah-blah." However, when they keep talking, the customer begins to hear the individual words: "Blah-blah morning. Welcome to Freddy's. Please let me know if I can help you find what you need."

Train your staff to pay attention to the signs that they have captured their audience. "Good morning. Welcome to Freddy's" may be enough. Sometimes, though, it takes many more words to get the message across. Prepare you and your staff with an armory of greetings so they have plenty to say. Encourage conversation and making connections. It pays off in the long run.

Do you know why "have a nice day" and "please come again" became such widespread, well-used closing comments? It's simple. "Bye" and "good-night" lack enough syllables for the message to sink in that you're making the effort to be polite and wish them a good evening so they will return.

Remember the importance of creating "Signature Moments"? Consider your parting comment another chance to create a Signature Moment.

Use the power of multiple syllables to let your customers know you really enjoy the fact they came in and spent time with you, and you're looking forward to doing business again. Sometimes it's actually appropriate to say all of that. Sometimes "have a nice day" will work, if delivered graciously and with sincerity, in a framework of rapport that is clearly devoted to that one individual.

More effective still is the added personal touch: "Make sure you enjoy this gorgeous day before the rain comes in this afternoon." "I hope you get all your errands done. If you need anything else, we're here for you."

Practice listening and paying attention to the snippets of information

Exceptional Care for Your Valued Client

your customer gives you about herself and her lifestyle, and use what you pick up on to add that personal touch to your closing comments.

Imprint a Signature Moment on your customer as he leaves. "If you decide to catch that movie, you can park in the lot around the corner for 50 cents an hour." "Thank you for coming in today. We get a shipment of new inventory from the brand you like every Wednesday, so I hope we get to see you again in a few days."

Be aware that you can get too comfortable with familiar customers and make huge mistakes when you just think you're being friendly. LuAnn tells a cautionary tale of a server in a well-known, upscale restaurant who made a serious, albeit well-intentioned faux pas. She got so friendly that she failed to realize she stepped over the line between client and staff.

LuAnn has a friend who adores this restaurant, and invites clients to dine there frequently. She enjoys being greeted by name, being seated at the best table, and being treated like royalty whenever she is there. The restaurant's reputation draws people from outrageous distances, and this woman enjoys being known to be known by the establishment. The way she is treated has a psychological impact on her clients; it reinforces the value of knowing and doing business with her, and it reinforces the fact that doing business with her is desirable.

One night she brought a new set of clients into the restaurant. It was extremely busy and the wait staff was obviously being kept on their toes. LuAnn's friend was greeted like an old friend and taken quickly to a table that had just been made available. It was still in the process of being re-set, though, and imagine her horror when a passing server called her by name and casually tossed her some silverware for the table. Suddenly the relationship changed, as did the way her clients saw her. The server may have thought this was a pleasant, social gesture. It was anything but. It was terribly disrespectful and embarrassing.

There is a definite line between treating your customer like an old friend and treating her like an employee. Asking your customer to do your job

Section 5

for you is crossing that line, and leaves a very sour taste in the customer's mouth, no matter how well you sugar-coat the request.

Respectful Elegance and having a Framework of Rapport enables you to ask anything of your customers, and I caution you to make sure your requests are within the bounds of respect.

You may see this gesture as friendly and inclusive, but step around the circle just a bit. You're asking your customer to pay for your services, right? When you ask them to take part in their own customer service it defeats the purpose of paying someone else to do the job. There's a reason LuAnn's friend takes her clients out to dinner instead of hosting parties at her home or catering events at other venues. She wants to show that she is special, and that she believes her guests are special, and being waited on is part of that experience for her. Being asked to help set the table takes the charm out of going to a high-end restaurant.

Remember that there is no exceptional care without service. Exceptional Care is a verb. You must always be in service mode. While you are at work, you are "on." When you are out in public, if you are lucky you will be recognized, and if you are wise, you will be "on." Use all the tools in the kit if you need to, just make sure you get yourself and keep yourself in that mind-set. You can indulge other attitudes and behaviors behind closed doors when you clock out for the day.

LuAnn recently decided to apply for a home equity line of credit (HELOC) and decided to do her research by physically going to three different banks to find the best match for her needs. "All three banks had roughly the same products to offer. The first two banks were pleasant enough, and were happy to give me the paperwork I needed. Pleasantly, they invited me back when I was done filling it all out.

"The third bank set itself apart in a couple of ways. When I walked in I was greeted by the most delicious smell of cookies baking – actually baking – somewhere in the bank. Cookies fresh out of the oven! Talk about building an instant framework of rapport. I had a cozy, happy feeling about these people right away. I think sometimes we accept that

Exceptional Care for Your Valued Client

large or busy institutions are cold and anonymous by default. Someone in that corporation had taken the time to think about what it's like to stand in line in a bank, and to find a way to make it enjoyable.

"What really clinched it for me, cookies or no cookies, was that at this bank an agent walked me to his desk, pulled out the paperwork, and filled it out for me. He asked me all the necessary questions, clarifying what needed clarifying, and taking the time to work with me then and there. He took the tedious and intimidating out of filling out the HELOC paperwork. It was an easy, natural service that made sense for them to provide, yet it made all the difference for me, a busy professional. That right there earned my business and my loyalty. And I had to wonder why the other banks made the decision to eliminate the service in the first place."

LuAnn conducts customer service seminars all over the country, and one question inevitably comes up in one form or another:

"How do I treat customers from other cultures? How do I treat customers from the Middle East, or Asia?" The question reveals a concern that different cultures have different customs, and there is a very real fear that an innocent comment or mannerism will offend and alienate the other person. In some cultures making eye contact is a sign of respect.

In other cultures, it is rude to look a stranger in the eye. In the United States, customers generally form lines and stand one behind the other, keeping the order they arrived in by physically placing themselves behind the person who was already in place. In other countries it is more common to stand in around in a group, keeping tabs on who came in what order without forming a line.

"With a little research you could learn and try to master all the nuances and signs of respect of all or most of the different cultures around the globe," says LuAnn. "However, I remind my clients that the world is so much smaller, and the world's cultures are so mixed and varied that there is no way to assume that you know enough about a customer's background to be congruent when you step out of your comfort zone to serve them the way you think is what they want. Especially in the US,

Section 5

people who are born and raised in the same cities and suburbs you were raised in can appear to be from another country, but culturally you're the same. You just cause yourself more problems."

LuAnn emphasizes the universal cues as the fool-proof tools for delivering exceptional service. "The tools in Remember the Ice make sense across the board. It's hard to offend anyone when you have a warm smile, a pleasant attitude of helpfulness, show that you are listening and paying attention, and have genuine interest in satisfying the customer. That comes through more loudly and clearly than anything else."

And if you do make a mistake? "Apologize. Then continue working to create a solution that will best benefit your customer. In all things, demonstrate respect. Remember ours is a global community and we all respond to being treated with respect whether we're used to the form it takes or it's a new experience. Let that guide your behavior; that is your safest bet."

LuAnn's final comment on the subject is the admonition to be aware of when you are stereotyping. "Learn to recognize when it's happening and change your mind-set to treat each person as an individual. Employ respectful elegance regardless of sex, race, religion, dress, height, weight, age or anything else."

Finally, there's one more old-fashioned practice that is coming back into style. For some of us it never went out of style, but across the board the art of the Thank You card has fallen by the wayside.

The hand-written Thank You card is the ultimate personal touch. "At the very least, send your client an e-mail or make a phone call," instructs LuAnn. "Take the time to reach out and express your gratitude for their business afterwards. It's a way to make contact and remind your client of you and your services without asking for business. It is pure appreciation. Of course it serves another purpose: It places you and your business squarely in front of them again – always an ideal practice. But that's secondary to the good old-fashioned purpose: Saying thank you, and meaning it."

Exceptional Care for Your Valued Client

LuAnn stresses the importance of hand-written messages. "Ideally, you will make the time to sit down and write out your thank you notes like your mother told you. The act of doing this forces you to sit quietly with your thoughts about the exchange between you and your customer. It feels good to remember a happy experience, and when your client reads the note, he too will re-experience the satisfaction of doing business with you, and will re-attach positive feelings with you and your company."

The thank you card is another way to spend more time with your existing customers without nagging them to death about doing business with you. "You want to 'touch' your customers several times to remind them that your alive," LuAnn says, "but too many e-mails, newsletters, special promotions and other advertisements flooding their inboxes can have the opposite effect than you want; too much of a good thing can be a bad thing and end up alienating your customer. A thank you note is courteous and has no strings attached. And it's always a nice touch."

"Send a thank you note for their business on a specific occasion, and make sure you send one for every referral you receive. It is empowering for your client to realize that he has guided a friend or associate to a professional who can meet his needs with confidence and class. Your client looks good for 'being in the know,' and that pride reinforces his good feelings about doing business with you in the first place. Yet another win-win."

If you struggle with what to say in a thank you note, keep it simple. There is Power in the Clarity of Your Articulation. "Thank you for your business" is a very good start, and begs to be included. A detail that is specific to that client is important:

- I'm glad that we were able to complete the project early so that you could fly up for your daughter's graduation. I'm sure it was a truly memorable weekend. Congratulations, again, on her achievement.

- I appreciate your patience while we tracked down the right color for you, and have been pleased to see your flags at the last three events

Section 5

downtown. That red really is striking. I keep an eye open for it every time I'm out enjoying the city, and point it out to whomever I am with.

- I'm so pleased that we were able to find a solution that worked for you, and that you were able to find some peace of mind in difficult times.

- We enjoyed having Rufus hang out in the office with us while we finished up the paperwork. He's a great dog, and we look forward to another visit from him soon.

- I'd also like to thank you for recommending the new coffee house to me. It is my new favorite place for coffee and pastries.

Whatever you come up with, make sure it is sincere, legible, and void of any (k)nots. A thank you note is the last thing you want tangled up with confusing messages.

Your motivation for providing exceptional care for your valued client must be pure. From the initial greeting to the thank you that sums your business up, each piece of your communication package must be steeped in a genuine drive to deliver the best product, best service, and best experience possible.

Stepping up your customer service game because you need an edge in a challenging economy, or because you are afraid of becoming another one of its victims, is counter-productive. Fear is never a good motivator. Fear is disempowering. Enthusiasm is empowering. Joy is empowering. Gratitude is empowering. Hope is empowering. Helpfulness is empowering. The more you practice these empowering mind-sets, the stronger and more powerful your customer service skills will become.

You must tap back into the passion and excitement that drove you to create your business in the first place, back when it was all you could think and dream about. Close your eyes and take yourself there. What really turned you on about your business? Is it still there? Can it light that fire in you again, after all this time?

Exceptional Care for Your Valued Client

Remember how you felt when the thrill of starting a new job merged with a new-found confidence in what you were doing, and sharing it with customers made you feel happy, powerful and effective? Those feelings are tremendously empowering. Life can get busy and those feelings can diminish if we let them. The key is to recapture that feeling and let it carry you through your days. Examining your thoughts and feelings through the process of the ABCs of Emotion can help re-ignite the old flame and keep the fire burning.

Use the tools in this book to rediscover your passion for *Providing Exceptional Care for Your Valued Client*. Use them to uncover the latent skills in employees who appear to have missed the boat when it comes to natural charm and just need direction and permission to indulge in how good it feels to succeed with people. Use them to discover and encourage the creative talents and unique perspective of each person you rely on to work with the public. This book is full of invisible values" layered beneath those that are spelled out for you. The more you practice what I preach, the more those layers will peel back and reveal themselves to you.

One of my core values is paying good forward. The good that my concepts do out in the world drives me to keep teaching, learning, speaking, writing, producing and sharing. I take my skills and do what I can to strengthen my relationships and my community. I am always excited to hear how the principles of Remember the Ice open the door to miracles and mind-blowing changes in individual businesses; and I am thrilled beyond measure when I hear stories of how those same business owners take these tools and apply them to doing what I call "The Next Right Thing," and end up changing their own relationships and communities in positive ways.

The next chapter is all about "The Next Right Thing." My hope is that the final message in this book will serve as a launching pad for new beginnings in your life and business.

Section 5

Chapter 20

The Next Logical Step: Doing the Next Right Thing

Providing Exceptional Care for Your Valued Client is a practice that is surprisingly simple to cultivate in yourself and in others. It requires knowledge, know-how, action, vigilance and the desire to do it in the first place.

The principles behind what I teach are sound. They make sense, so they're easy to remember and adopt. And they're powerful. Based on the feedback I've been getting for the past 40 years, even the tiny changes make giant impacts. Dramatic changes can have mind-boggling results.

Good word choice leads to good results; empowering word choice leads to empowering results.

Providing Exceptional Care for Your Valued Client is just the beginning. The limit of your influence is in your hands. When you have a solid foundation supporting your words and actions, you can impact the world around you in ever-expanding circles of success.

Now that you have the tools you need to succeed with your customers and clients, it's time to really ramp up your new-found power and put it to even better use. This is what I call doing "The Next Right Thing" and it has everything to do with the good that comes back to you when you send your good out into the universe.

Remember when I talked about how important it is to include *expecting good* in your mind-set in order to demonstrate the congruence that is so necessary to effective communication? The reason is that when you think, speak and act with good in mind, you and your message are infinitely more powerful than when you have other motives.

Doing the next right thing is basically acting on the conscious decision to look for and choose a positive, productive outlet for the

Exceptional Care for Your Valued Client

empowerment you have achieved for yourself. For the purpose of this book I'm going to share three areas where the Exceptional Care tools you have picked up here can have a powerful impact for good. It's more than going above and beyond, it's taking a physical step to the next right thing to do.

In leadership, it's the difference between explaining why texting at the customer service desk is wrong, and instituting a policy where each employee's phone – including yours – is to stay off the sales floor and safely locked up in the office.

Leadership is a trait that can be demonstrated among co-workers on the same level; no one's job is too small, too entry-level, or too part-time to exclude leadership behavior.

On the floor, Philip is one of the best customer service representatives the company has ever had. He is animated and charming, responsive and attentive. In no time at all, he has people eating out of his hands. He makes eye contact, remembers names and small details about each person, matches the need with the right product, and makes sure his customers go home happy and feeling good about their purchases.

It is obvious that this is deeply satisfying to Philip. He lights up when customers walk into the store, and positively hums when he's working with them.

Philip's co-workers marvel at his skill and surreptitiously observe "how he does it" in order to try to emulate him.

Working with a customer on the phone, however, is an entirely different matter. Philip will do just about anything to avoid answering an incoming call, including feigning ignorance that the phone is ringing at all. By unspoken consent, the rest of the team let him answer the phone only as a last resort.

Watching Philip answer the phone one morning Gerry, a co-worker and good friend, winces. She is tied up with another customer and is unable

Section 5

to answer it. The phone rings several times, and only after another salesperson asks him to take the call does Philip move towards it. His shoulders slump and out of nowhere his energy level slumps and he becomes dark and discouraged, almost as if a black cloud looms over his head.

He picks up the phone, brings it up to his face as if it weighs a ton, and mumbles some indistinct and uninterested greeting that even Gerry has a hard time understanding. He grunts a few times, gives a half-literate answer to a question, repeats himself a few times without clarifying, then hangs up.

The first time Gerry witnessed this behavior she was aghast. She watched the manager pull him aside and heard him lecture about speaking clearly, sounding cheerful, and being helpful on the phone. Philip had nodded like he understood. He had now nodded like he understood after two succeeding lectures that had failed to have an effect on his behavior, and it was clearly annoying their manager.

Armed with the tools from this book, Gerry is riding on the waves of her own success. Her customer service skills have grown by leaps and bounds, and her customer satisfaction ranks highest in the store. In sales, she is catching up to Philip and will soon surpass him. She thinks about it and decides to do the next right thing and apply her tools to try to help her friend's phone presence, if he would let her.

She thought about her word choice as well as the signs of congruency in communication; she would watch for them in herself and in Philip, to see what he was responding to and what he was pretending to respond to. She also thought about what she understood of the ABCs of Emotion and Circling the Situation. Considering the dramatic personality change in Philip between face-to-face customer interaction and working with someone on the phone, she figured something else had to be going on here.

On their lunch break, Gerry tells him what a great salesperson she thinks he is, and mentions a few skills that genuinely impress her. Then she gets to the point.

Exceptional Care for Your Valued Client

"Philip, you are a completely different person when you talk on the phone. It's like night and day; it's like you hate the person calling or the fact that they called or something," she says. "What's that about?"

Philip shrugs, "I've never been good on the phone. I like to text or e-mail. Or Facebook. You know that."

"Yeah, but you're so good with people. They love you. What's the deal with talking to them on the phone? It's the same thing, just without them here, that's all."

Philip shakes his head and puts down his sandwich. "No. It's different. If they were really interested, they'd come down to the store. When they get here, they're a real person. They made the effort to get here so I make the effort to help them."

Gerry laughs. "That sounds nothing like you. Seriously? You only think they're worth the trouble if they got off their couch and came down here?"

"Well, no," Philip shifts uneasily in his chair. "Okay, you want to know what it is?"

Gerry nods. She is listening more carefully than she shows.

"When you have someone standing in front of you, you can tell what they're thinking. Like, if they're seriously interested or just kicking tires. I can see what's important to them, like if I start talking about speed and their eyes glaze over I switch to details or something until I can tell they're into it," Philip explains. "Then I can figure out what's most important to them and guide them to what they need. I like doing that."

Ah. Body language cues. Physiology; that's what Philip understands.

"So when you're on the phone it's hard to tell if you're leading them in the right direction or wasting their time?" Gerry asks.

"Yeah, that's it," Philip perks up. "That's exactly it. It's impossible to

Section 5

know what they're thinking when it's just their voice."

Gerry chews for a minute, then says, "It's actually pretty clear, you just have to know what to listen for."

Philip snorts. "Says you."

"Yeah, says me. It's all about tone of voice. Like you learned that eyes glazing over means losing interest, a tone of voice or a sigh or suddenly going quiet can say that, too. You just have to learn verbal cues."

"Learn verbal cues? That sounds like work. And I never learned about eyes glazing over, I just always knew it," Philip scoffs.

"Yes you did. You learned it when you were a little kid, too young to remember or know what was going on. So now you just have to pay attention and learn what the different things you're hearing mean. If a little kid can do it, you can do it," she adds.

"Okay, professor," Philip teases, "how am I supposed to do that? You teaching classes you forgot to tell me about?"

"Very funny. Here's what you do. Simple. You barely have to think about it when a guy's body language changes, right? So for like the rest of today pay attention to those changes and really listen to what their voice is doing. Even if you're talking, pay attention to the sighs and the silences, and when you get interrupted. Just pay attention to what happens and then make a note of it.

Then, when you're on the phone, practice listening and react like you would if you heard that cue in a real body in front of you and picture how that sound or silence goes with what body language. Maybe you'll get it wrong a couple of times, but you'll catch on and then you'll be the master of the sales floor again, and I will have to give you a run for your money. Again," Gerry says with a wink.

Philip thinks about it. "Yeah, alright. I can do that. You're getting a bit

Exceptional Care for Your Valued Client

too big for your britches anyway, so I'm going to like getting better than you at yet one more thing."

Rather than keeping her new-found tools for success to herself and outshining her friend, Gerry chose to do the next right thing and share a helpful idea with him. Within a short amount of time Philip finds himself having fun figuring out the mysterious cues coming from the other end of the phone. His success is the store's success, and the task of answering the phone is finally allotted evenly among the entire team.

Doing the next right thing in leadership is also about paying attention when you hire, place and schedule employees. Using your skills to take the next step beyond training your staff to practice the principles of providing exceptional care for your valued client translates fluidly into moving people out of positions that are unsuccessful for them and into positions that take full advantage of their skills and natural abilities.

Placing your people in roles where they are confident, interested, curious and energized translates into happy, productive and successful employees. When they thrive, the business thrives. When they wilt, guess what? Your customers know it, and your business wilts.

I classify this action as a "next right thing" because it can be much easier to replace employees, especially in high-turnover industries, than it is to find or create jobs that are more suited to their individual personalities. However, the return on investment when you do just that can be quite large.

If Philip was unable to learn how to work with customers over the phone, redesigning his job may have been the only alternative. A possible solution would be to replace phone answering duties with employee training duties. His obvious talent with people, coupled with his co-workers' obvious interest in emulating that talent, would make a powerful combination.

There are countless ways to do the next right thing within your business. The possibilities for combining efforts to work together with other businesses like the ones that came up with the printer and the event

Section 5

sponsor are also beyond limit. Doing the next right thing is literally taking action to do something good with the tools I have given you here.

The next right thing extends beyond where you work, who you work with and who you partner with. It extends into the community, into networking and fund-raising, and into creating something solid and good that has purpose. The principles behind Remember the Ice work together for productive good. Applied to your dreams, they change your life. Applied to your life, they change your world.

Take a look at your life, at where you live and work, and think about what kind of positive change you can make, and take that action; do that next right thing.

For my wife Nancy and I, doing the next right thing came in the form of creating The Life is For Giving Foundation. We established this organization to fulfill the final wishes of adults with terminal illnesses. We manage it one person at a time, and draw on our network and resources of friends and business associates to help make each dream come true. Our purpose has always been to give back, or rather to pay forward the blessings we have received. We have been tricked. In the course of paying blessings forward, we find we receive more than we could ever have anticipated.

The sheer joy of fulfilling a final wish is beyond anything we had ever imagined. The people who help us create the experience come back to us without fail deeply touched, flush with joy, hoping for more opportunities to make a difference. And so we, and they, continue to give. And continue to receive.

That is the secret. That is the *"why"* behind making the choice to take your tools of empowerment and choosing to do a next right thing that is bigger than you; when you give, you receive tenfold.

The great lesson of this book, the very point of it, is that when you give, you receive. LuAnn and I are members of BNI, the world's largest business networking organization. In BNI it is called "Givers Gain" and

Exceptional Care for Your Valued Client

it is one of the foundational philosophies behind its leadership and success. We live, behave and teach to this principle, to our continued success.

Providing *Exceptional Care for Your Valued Client* is an act of giving. So, give. Then pay attention to what you receive. Then give some more. One feeds the other. This is one of the most powerful laws in the universe.

It may feel strange at first to put into practice what we've been talking about in this book, to untie the (k)nots in your language, to make the effort to choose the perfect word instead of a good-enough word, to deliberately change your expression to a smile before answering the phone, to "set the stage" in your place of business for someone else's comfort, and to listen compassionately to a customer whom you would rather show the door, but remember: That's the way new behaviors are supposed to feel until they become habit and instinct.

There is power in the clarity of your articulation. The extent to which you choose to employ the tools provided for you has a direct bearing on your success. Your commitment to using them is up to you. Your success is up to you.

Section 5

SECTION 5 Exercises

Where Do You Go From Here?
Accountability & Action Create the Paradigm

To borrow a simple action phrase from fellow speaker Tony Wolfe, "Go Do!"

Nike's moniker shouts the message: "Just Do It"

The exercises suggested here are reviewed in the text below from Chapter 19. Let's revisit for a moment.

Use the tools in this book to rediscover your passion for *Exceptional Care for Your Valued Client.* Use them to uncover the latent skills in employees who appear to have missed the boat when it comes to natural charm and just need direction and permission to indulge in how good it feels to succeed with people. Use them to discover and encourage the creative talents and unique perspective of each person you rely on to work with the public. This book is full of "invisible values" layered beneath those that are spelled out for you. The more you practice what I preach, the more those layers will peel back and reveal themselves to you.

One of my core values is paying good forward. The good that my concepts do out in the world drives me to keep teaching, learning, speaking, writing, producing and sharing. I take my skills and do what I can to strengthen my relationships and my community. I am always excited to hear how the principles of Remember the Ice open the door to miracles and mind-blowing changes in individual businesses. And I am thrilled beyond measure when I hear stories of how those same business owners take these tools and apply them to doing what I call "The Next Right Thing," and end up changing their own relationships and communities in positive ways.

So peel the layers back; Go do the Next Right Thing; and take off from your launching pad in providing *Exceptional Care for Your Valued Client.*

Oh, and please share your stories.
Email me at **bob.nicoll@remembertheice.com**

Exceptional Care for Your Valued Client

Biographies

Bob Nicoll, M.A.

Symphonies are created one individual note at a time. They are composed with care and craft, the notes placed according to their qualities to soften the melody or strengthen the rising rush of music. A word, standing alone, is as full of potential as a single note. Just as it is with notes in a symphony, where that single word is placed among other words lends it strength, clarity and purpose.

There is power in the clarity of your articulation. ™

When Bob composed this message, the words came easily. For almost 40 years he has nurtured a passion for linguistics and empowering word choice; more specifically, the juxtaposition of words. After completing his B.S. in Psychology in 1972, and Masters in Counseling in 1974 he focused his energies on studying the power of word choice: The Psychophysiology of Words. He refined his skills working with leading personal growth and development leaders over the next 20 years while earning certifications in Rational Behavior Therapy and Neuro-Associative Conditioning Systems.

He has been a counseling psychologist, business owner, consultant, motivational speaker, sales trainer, restaurant owner, financial planner and a top sales manager. In each role he has consistently found opportunities to tap into his passion: *Helping people shift their paradigms with respect to empowering word choices.*

Remember the Ice helps you enhance your most important skill: communication with family members, friends, clients, co-workers — anyone who is important to you. It helps you stay focused on your task and accomplish your goals because you are conveying your message, and articulating your thoughts in a clear, precise manner. You eliminate confusion and gain confidence in your message and ultimately attract more of what you want.

Exceptional Care for Your Valued Client

Bob and his wife Nancy live in Eagle River, just outside Anchorage, Alaska and have three adult children and twin grandchildren. His passions include travel, photography, golf and *"helping shift people's paradigms"*. Since 1991, when he created Remember the Ice, he has honed his articulation skills and developed his innovative program. In October 2008, his first book **Remember the Ice and Other Paradigm Shifts** was released and has been received on a global scale, with copies in 38 countries.

Exceptional Care for Your Valued Client is the second in the Remember the Ice series.

Biographies

LuAnn Buechler, CMP, M.S.

LuAnn Buechler has been in the hospitality industry for more than 30 years. She has worked in all areas of the hotel industry including holding management positions in banquets, convention services, catering and sales. In 2003 she earned her Master's Degree in Hospitality Administration and became an Adjunct Professor teaching Meeting and Convention Management at the University of Wisconsin, Stout.

LuAnn is also a Certified Meeting Professional (CMP), and has carried this designation for 12 years. In this capacity she recently supervised an office of 28 individuals responsible for planning medical meetings for physicians at the Mayo School of Continuing Medical Education, at the Mayo Clinic in Rochester, MN.

As an Independent Professional Meeting Consultant, LuAnn operates her own successful business, PMC Events and Travel.

When LuAnn joined Business Network International (BNI), she realized immediately that word-of-mouth marketing was the best way to grow her business. Other than her website, **www.PMCEvents.com**, it is the only way she chooses to market her business. Her key to success is: Relationships, Relationships, Relationships!

Now a director for BNI, LuAnn has built a repertoire of presentations on networking skills and relationship marketing which she applies to delivering high quality customer service. She believes that caring is the ultimate competitive advantage, and delivers customer service training with the same passion that she delivers customer service in her own event management business.

LuAnn uses her unique personality and rich history of experience to deliver presentations that inspire people to achieve the success they

Exceptional Care for Your Valued Client

desire in business and in life. LuAnn is genuinely inspired by inspiring others. LuAnn takes great pride in serving others first and lives by the BNI philosophy "Givers Gain."

As a Certified Facilitator of "The Passion Test," LuAnn shares with audiences the simple yet powerful SYSTEM (Saving Your Self Time Energy & Money) used to determine each individual's true passions and help set a course for living his or her life's destiny.

Passionate about everything she does, LuAnn is also a part of the Transformational Leadership Council (TLC) working team. TLC is an organization created by Jack Canfield, best-selling co-author of the "Chicken Soup for the Soul" series, where transformational leaders share best practices and co-create humanitarian projects to transform the world.

LuAnn is the creator of the Get Connected Conference series. This event covers several days and is designed to provide valuable, practical entrepreneurial education from some of the most noteworthy and successful experts in the networking field to those business professionals who conduct a significant amount of their business through word-of-mouth or referral marketing. Presenters focus exclusively on how business can *survive and* **thrive** in any challenging economic environment.

When Bob sat down to write a book that would take his empowering and life-changing concepts from "Remember the Ice and Other Paradigm Shifts" and apply them to providing **Exceptional Care for Your Valued Clients**, he turned to LuAnn. By sharing her wisdom and experience with Bob and Bronwyn, her extensive contributions have helped bring depth, meaning and insight to its pages.

Biographies

Bronwyn Emery Ashbaker

Bronwyn Emery Ashbaker is a freelance writer with editing experience who specializes in providing professional copy for valued clients with a variety of needs, including web-site content, press releases, grants, newsletters, marketing tools, articles, speeches, business documents, presentations, outlines, biographies, and books. She brings to the table experience in promotions development, multimedia communications, publications management and direct consumer communications. Bob and Bronwyn have collaborated on a number of projects directly related to his breakthrough program, "Remember the Ice." As Bob's developmental editor, friend, and student, Bronwyn has had countless opportunities to apply the principles of empowering word choice to her own life as a mother, consultant, writer and customer service agent. As a professional writer, she was hesitant to drop "not" from her language, but quickly discovered the power and practicality of being clear and direct, especially with her teenage children.

Bob and Bronwyn first worked together in 2007 at Alaska Professional Sports, Inc., where her responsibilities as the Marketing and Community Relations Director were focused on the inaugural season of the Indoor Football League team "Alaska Wild." She prepared press releases, articles, biographies, newsletters, game-day scripts, speeches and specific program and web-site content. Her role also included planning, outlining and coordinating game-day, corporate and media events, developing, managing and directing game day operations relating to entertainment, promotions and public announcements, and working with sales, entertainers, coaches, operations and arena management to develop each game-day and event script.

Prior to her involvement with the Alaska Wild, Bronwyn was an editor and columnist at the Tracy Press, one of the last independent

Exceptional Care for Your Valued Client

newspapers in California. In her time at the Tracy Press, she developed and maintained a unique weekly community newspaper section, "Our Town," that quickly grew from six to 32 pages and became a brand within the community, one of the anchors of which was her weekly column, "Connections."

Working with up to 30 contributors at a time, including interns, volunteer columnists from the community, and professional reporters and photographers, as the editor she was responsible for planning, assigning, editing and managing all content for the section, including stories, columns, reviews, art, calendars, captions, and miscellaneous copy.

Along with her column, Bronwyn enjoyed the life-changing experience of interviewing and sharing the story of a different local character each week. She had the opportunity to sit one-on-one with more than 200 people in five years, exploring with them the unique and wonderful in each individual. It changed the way she looks at the people in her life, and the people she passes on the street.

Although she has had many rich and diverse experiences working for other people, freelance writing has been a steady companion in one form or another – sometimes in the foreground, often in the background – for more than 10 years. She looks forward to collaborating with Bob and LuAnn on future projects.

CPSIA information can be obtained at www.ICGtesting.com
Printed in the USA
266936BV00001B/14/P